Praise f

OUT OF THE FIRE

"Well over a decade ago, as a college student, Mike shared his story with me as his unique life purpose was just becoming clear. I was deeply moved. Now, he is sharing it with all of you. Learn from it. It will inform the pursuit of your unique life purpose and you will be better for it. I guarantee it."

> —**Douglas R. Conant,** founder of ConantLeadership, *New York Times* and *Wall Street Journal* bestselling author, retired CEO of Campbell Soup Company, and former chairman of Avon Products

"I have known Mike Kinney since he was twelve years old. The night he was Life-Flighted to the hospital, I was there. Reading Mike's story brought back memories of his horrifying experience. When you live through an experience like that, you must decide if it's going to make you bitter or better—if it's going to cause you to blame God or see God. Mike has used his experience to make him better, to help him see God. And now he shares his story in order to help us see God as well. *Out of the Fire* will inspire you and encourage your faith."

> —**Steve Poe,** former lead pastor of Northview Church and author of *Creatures of Habit*

"*Out of the Fire* is outstanding! In fact, I read it in two sittings. In the season I'm facing today, I've been asking God 'Why me?' and 'What's next?' This book reassured me that as I walk through these difficult days, I can have faith that He will take care of me and my family. This book will be such a blessing to all who read it and will serve as a reminder that God keeps His promises to us—all we need to do is keep the faith in Him in all aspects of our lives."

  —Andrea Morehead Allen, former WTHR Channel 13 news
   anchor and author of *The Brightest Star*

"Each of us has circumstances and events in our lives that we would never choose. For Mike Kinney, it was a brutal automobile accident. Rescued from death, Mike searched for meaning. Where was God? Why had he suffered? What was his purpose? As you share this intimate journey through suffering and into hope, you just may find answers to some of those questions you've been asking about your own life."

  —Steve Arterburn, host of *New Life Live* and author
   of more than one hundred books, including *Every
   Believer's Thought Life*

Out of the Fire

MIKE KINNEY
with MARGOT STARBUCK

OUT
OF THE
FIRE

How an Angel *and* a Stranger
Intervened to Save a Life

SALEM
BOOKS
an imprint of Regnery Publishing
Washington, D.C.

Salem Books™ is a trademark of Salem Communications Holding Corporation.
Regnery® is a registered trademark and its colophon is a trademark of Salem Communications Holding Corporation.

Cataloging-in-Publication data on file with the Library of Congress

ISBN: 978-1-68451-273-7
eISBN: 978-1-68451-321-5

Library of Congress Control Number: 2022941039

Published in the United States by
Salem Books
An Imprint of Regnery Publishing
A Division of Salem Media Group
Washington, D.C.
www.SalemBooks.com

Manufactured in the United States of America

10 9 8 7 6 5 4 3 2 1

Books are available in quantity for promotional or premium use. For information on discounts and terms, please visit our website: www.SalemBooks.com.

For Jack, Henry, and baby Caroline.

It's the greatest blessing of my life to be your daddy.

*You are so deeply loved and created for a purpose
that is uniquely your own.*

I believe in you.

CONTENTS

PREFACE

In some of the most critical and terrifying moments of our lives, we naturally wonder if God is with us. The moment when I most needed to know that God was with me was when I was in a car crash as a teenager.

Since that time, I've met countless others who have wondered whether God was with them in their most difficult moments. A young woman who was adopted as an infant wondered if God was with her in the hospital in the minutes and hours after her delivery. A college student, currently wracked with despair and considering taking his life, wonders if God is present in his suffering. A wife trapped in an abusive relationship wonders if God sees her tears and hears her cries. A young father diagnosed with Stage 4 pancreatic cancer wonders if God is present in his anguish.

When our relationships rupture, when we suffer despair, weather abuse, or receive a terrifying diagnosis, we wonder if God is with us. We wonder if He sees us. We wonder if He hears us. We wonder if He cares.

My invitation, as I share my story with you, is to notice those seasons and moments of your own journey that are most tender. Ask God's Spirit to show you the hurt or moment or season in your life He longs to touch, to heal, to redeem. Pay attention to the old hurts that continue to bubble up. And look for the ways you feel stuck today.

Like my accident and the painful recovery that followed, as well as lasting effects that linger to this day, I suspect you never would have chosen to endure some of what you've experienced. And yet, these critical moments and seasons are the exact places where we have the opportunity to encounter the God who is with us and for us.

I met God in the fire, and I pray that you will encounter the presence of Jesus in the fiery seasons of your own journey. Maybe it's a moment from your past that's still smoldering. Or maybe you're feeling the heat today and are hungry to know that God is near. Join me on this journey so you might experience the powerful, redeeming presence of the One who is with you and for you.

CHAPTER 1

THE LAST THREE LAWNS

*D*ing!
 The text alert woke me up on the third day of school—
August 16, 2002. Unfortunately, it alerted my history teacher as well.

"Mr. Kinney, are you with us?" he asked.

All eyes in the room fell on me, and one guy from the swim team snickered under his breath.

"Yes, I'm here," was all I could think to say in my fatigued stupor. I silenced my phone, sliding it under my binder.

I'd been swimming five hours a day during summer workouts and had woken up that morning feeling under the weather. I was excited and nervous about what I hoped would be my best year of high school yet, but I wasn't starting strong. Willing myself to sit up straight in my chair, I glanced at the clock over the doorway. Just ten more minutes until early release, and then the weekend

1

would be mine. Thinking about the lawns I was scheduled to mow after school, I dutifully scribbled some notes as my teacher droned on.

Brrrnnnggg!

When the bell rang, I grabbed my phone, swept the contents of my desktop into my black canvas backpack, avoided my teacher's glare, and dipped out of class into a hallway pulsing with other students as eager to be liberated as I was.

Glancing down at my phone, I read the text. It was from Matt, a friend from church who went to a different school, Carmel High, not too far from mine outside of Indianapolis. We'd grown closer over the summer through a small group, but we hadn't seen each other since he'd gotten back that week from visiting family and surfing in California. Peeking at my watch, I knew Matt had also just gotten out of class.

I texted, "Can't wait to get out of here! I've got three lawns to mow. Help me knock 'em out and let's hang!" Matt had helped me mow before and we always split the pay.

Crossing the parking lot, I reached my fifteen-year-old red Ford Ranger truck just as a girl named Klancy from my chemistry class was pulling out of the space beside mine in her gray Honda Civic. Slipping between the vehicles, I raised a hand to let her know I saw her car moving. The August heat was turning everything into a steam bath, and I felt sweat begin to bead down the side of my face as I slid behind the wheel of my truck, rolled down the windows, and read Matt's reply.

Yeah, sounds good. Where?

The first job was my next-door neighbor, so I told Matt to meet at my house and dropped my phone into the open center console.

Michael W. Smith's song "Breathe" came blasting from my CD player when I turned the key.

I started backing slowly out of the parking spot to avoid hitting other teens checking their phones for messages, then stopped to let a group of kids pass behind my truck. One of them spotted the equipment I kept in the flatbed for my lawn-mowing business—a lawn mower, a hedge trimmer, some clippers, as well as a few cans of gas and oil—and called out, "Nice gear, Kinney!"

Josh McClain was the kind of bully other kids thought was cool. He got a few laughs from his friends for the remark, which is exactly what he was after. Unlike my ragtag mowing gigs, Josh actually ran a legit lawncare business. I pressed my lips together rather than barking back what I would have liked to say. I knew that other kids, even the ones who got bullied more than me, would have snapped back at him. Or at least muttered angry words to themselves. But I believed I shouldn't resist. So I let the remark go, ignored Josh and his posse, and kept moving.

I'd pulled into the concrete driveway alongside our 1970s tri-level home and was unloading my mower when Matt pulled up in his snazzy red Toyota Supra. With his windows down, the sounds of Dave Matthews Band blaring from the custom speakers he'd installed filled my neighborhood. I'd seen Matt take his car up to 120 mph before, and was grateful that he hadn't roared down my street like the speed demon he could be.

Matt parked along the curb in front of our home, hopped out and yelled, "Hey, bro!"

He was wearing shorts and an aqua T-shirt from some West Coast surf shop. I noticed he was tanner than he'd been two weeks earlier and his hair was lighter.

"So you catch some good waves?" I asked.

"You know I did!" he answered with a big goofy grin on his face.

When Matt got to my truck, I handed him the hedge trimmer.

"Okay, you start on those bushes," I instructed, pointing to the hedges lining my neighbor's brick ranch home, "and I'll start on the front lawn. Let's knock out these three jobs so we can grab some food."

The lawns took longer than I'd planned, but the money made it worthwhile. All three clients gave me checks I shoved into the glove box of my truck to deposit at the bank on Monday.

Matt knew I was scheduled to lead worship for our church's middle school youth group at six, so when we finished at 5:15, we headed toward Northview Church instead of our favorite fast-food joint—grub would just have to wait until after practice. I was a regular worship leader for the high school youth group, and that Friday night I was filling in for one of the middle school worship leaders who couldn't make it. Although Matt didn't play an instrument, he loved leading worship and was happy to join me as a singer.

By the time we'd finished the five songs in our set and the middle schoolers started playing arcade games around 6:45, we drove separately to our favorite restaurant; after that, we planned to check out the football game at Matt's school. As I scarfed down my two junior bacon cheeseburgers, I got to hear about Matt's surfing trip.

We got to Matt's high school around 8:15 and began trolling the crowded lot looking for parking spaces. When we finally headed toward the entrance to the field, the game was approaching halftime and we could hear the roar of cheering fans.

We beelined to the section where a lot of our friends from church were sitting. They greeted us with high fives as we slid into the stadium bleachers beside them.

As Carmel inched the ball down the field, Matt turned to me and suggested, "Hey, let's go to my lake house tonight."

The small lake property Matt's family owned was about a thirty-minute drive away.

"That sounds awesome," I agreed, making a mental note to call my mom when I was someplace that wasn't so noisy. Matt's parents and sister would be there, and the next day we could go jet skiing.

"I definitely need to stop for gas before we go to the lake," I announced, knowing if I didn't tell Matt, I'd likely forget.

We hadn't even been at the game fifteen minutes when Matt's phone rang. I didn't know who he was talking to, but I heard him say, "Yeah, cool. See you in a few." He clicked off and then turned to me.

"Remember I told you about Jenna, who worked at the car wash with me?" Matt asked.

I nodded. She was a girl I knew he'd been crushing on.

"Well, she and a few of her friends are at O'Charley's, and they want us to come. You in?"

Not only was I at some other school's football game where I knew few people, but…*girls*. So, *yeah*, I was in. I'd taken an interest in girls later than a lot of guys I knew, and I hadn't really dated anyone. So I was down for hanging out with some of Matt's friends. I gave a thumbs up to O'Charley's.

On the drive over I called my mom to ask if I could sleep at Matt's lake house. Reassured that his parents would be there, she gave me her blessing.

After finding parking at O'Charley's, Matt spotted Jenna and her friends through the window as we approached the door. Once in, we scooted into opposites sides of a booth made for six.

"Hey guys, this is my friend Mike," Matt said.

Feeling a little bit awkward, I said, "Hey, nice to meet you."

The girls went around the table and introduced themselves. As we all talked, it became clear that Matt's flirting game was much stronger than mine.

When the waitress approached the table to take our order, I balked. Our burger run before the game had almost wiped me out, and I'd spent my last three bucks getting into the stadium. And I knew Matt didn't have very much money.

"What can I get you?" she asked politely, looking back and forth between Matt and me.

"Uhhh…" Matt hedged. "I think I'll start with a glass of water, please."

Taking his cue, I agreed, "Me, too. Water, please. Thanks."

We were pretty classy.

Matt and I hung out with the girls as they finished their meals. At about 10:15 p.m., we all left, and Matt and I headed toward his family's lake house, agreeing to stop on US-31 to get gas.

After sliding into a parking spot alongside the gas station, Matt walked over to the pump to find me scrounging through my truck looking for gas money.

"Shoot," I exclaimed. "Can I borrow some money, man? My truck will not make it much further and I don't have any cash."

Matt opened up his empty wallet, flashing it in my direction.

Digging both of his hands into his front pockets, he pulled out a wadded-up bill. As I watched him unfold it, I quietly hoped it was going to be more than one dollar.

Matt raised it and triumphantly exclaimed, "Five bucks!" as if he'd just won the lottery.

Five bucks would get me almost four gallons. Snatching the bill from Matt's hand, I headed inside and slid it across the counter to the cashier smacking her gum.

"Five bucks on Pump Two, please."

"Do you need a receipt?" the woman asked.

"Nah," I said, "thanks."

As I squeezed the pump handle, Matt and I talked about Jenna. When four dollars and seventy cents rolled by on the monitor, I loosened my grip to slow the flow of gas in an effort to hit five dollars on the nose.

Stopping at four dollars and ninety-nine cents, I gave the slightest squeeze, and was crushed when I saw the price roll over to $5.01. Though I knew we could most likely turn up a penny in one of our cars, it was still a blow to my adolescent ego. I opened my driver-side door, where I found a single penny tucked under the carpet.

I picked it up and humbly took it inside to the cashier. I knew some of my buddies on the swim team would have just driven away, but doing the right thing had been ingrained in me since I was a child. My dad was an elder at our church, and I was serious about my own faith. I'd made that decision when I was nine, and had been growing in my faith since then. I was also just naturally that kind of conscientious kid who just wanted to do the right thing.

Matt and I flipped on our headlights and pulled back onto US-31 N. I noticed a few cop cars that had pulled drivers over as we passed. I suspected that speedy Matt had noticed them, too, because he wasn't gunning it the way he usually did. I followed his red sports car as he turned onto East 236th Street, a straight route with dipping slopes that would take us to the lake.

The first few miles were darkened by thick groves of trees with branches overhanging the highway, but when we emerged into wide-open corn and soybean farmland, the moon lit up the gently rolling fields. That's where we got stuck behind three slow cars on the narrow two-lane road. If it had been just one, I know Matt would have passed it. But since it was three, we dutifully stayed in our lane. I still felt physically wiped out from swim practice and was happy to mindlessly follow his taillights. With no stop signs or traffic lights to slow us down, I kept the truck in fifth gear.

Matt's rearview mirror was catching the glare of my headlights, so he reached forward to tilt it down to dim the shine. But noticing a sudden movement of the previously unwavering beams in that reflection, Matt looked up to see my truck swerving back and forth across the road.

I, however, was completely unaware.

CHAPTER 2

BLAZING INFERNO

Matt looked up to see my car swerving across the road, crossing the divider line, and rumbling across the gravelly shoulder toward a ditch, and then swerving back into my own lane. To his eye, no one was in control of the vehicle. Before he had time to react, Matt saw my truck swerve again and careen off the road completely.

The front of my truck was protected by large black brush guards. This protective steel feature, which looks a little like the grill on a football helmet, is meant to protect the headlights and other front-end features of the truck, and in a major head-on collision, it's meant to absorb some of the initial shock of impact.

After barreling through roadside vegetation, my truck plowed straight into, and through, a dead tree that had been hollowed out by termites. The force of the impact sent the truck heading back toward the road and off the left side of the road, scraping against a six-foot-high cement block and then crashing into a telephone pole. Though 1987 Ford trucks have notably long hoods, in an instant mine crumpled all the way to the dashboard, collapsing on top of my legs.

Matt slammed his brakes and made a quick U-turn, then stopped and jumped out of his car. The chaos Matt encountered appeared a lot like that left behind by a tornado: branches and bark were strewn across the soybean field where I'd crashed. One twisted lawn mower, a hedge trimmer, and two gas cans littered the bare ground beside a big grove of trees.

Because my truck had smashed into the telephone pole on my side, Matt wisely ran to the opposite door. Through the window, he could see me slumped against my seat belt—and flames on the passenger-side floorboard beginning to spread throughout the truck. Yanking at the door handle, he found it locked, so he braced his arm and slammed his elbow into the glass in an attempt to break it. When that failed, he kicked at the window, but his shoe, damp from the grass, slid right off.

Avoiding the flaming front end of the truck, Matt dashed around the back and opened my door with his left hand. He put his hands under my arms and pulled with all his strength. At a lean five-feet seven-inches tall, and with the truck's dipping at an odd angle into the ditch, it was difficult to get any leverage. My body didn't budge.

Matt suddenly saw that my seatbelt was still buckled. Reaching across my body, which was already being burnt by the flames licking at my legs, he unbuckled my seatbelt, placed his arms under mine, and again yanked as hard as he could. But my unconscious body still wouldn't budge.

"Help!" Matt screamed into the darkness. "Help! Help! Help!" No cars were passing by.

With his chin on my shoulder, Matt angled my upper body out of the truck, but my legs were still pinned under the dash. My brown leather Sketchers offered some protection for my feet, but the flames coming from the floorboard under the pedals were climbing up my legs, burning through my jeans. The inside of the cab was lit up against the dark night sky.

"Jesus," Matt begged, "You have to help me. Help me Jesus, please help me!"

He continued to tug on my limp body, to no avail. Fire was coming out of the truck's hood, and the gearshift area was also on fire. It was still eighty degrees outside, and with each moment the truck was getting hotter and hotter. Sweat poured off Matt's brow, and dark soot clung to his body and clothes as he wrestled for my life.

Matt couldn't tell whether I was alive or dead until he heard me make a gurgling sound, like I was choking.

Despite being the only human in sight, Matt had the palpable sense of another presence with him. He felt there was an angel in the cab, bearing silent witness. And when he glanced at the passenger seat, there was a clearing where no smoke hovered, as if the physical space was occupied by a being he couldn't see. The angel wasn't helping in a physically tangible way, but the awareness of it calmed Matt's heart as he continued to wrestle to free me.

Ring!

The sound of Matt's cell phone in his pocket startled him. Without looking to see who the caller was, he instinctively answered, said, "Super serious accident!" and hung up.

For his entire life, Matt had been obsessed with rescue workers, paramedics, and firefighters. In sixth grade he announced to his parents that he wanted to be a doctor. But in this moment, even though he had a phone in his pocket, Matt hadn't thought to call 9-1-1. Instead, his body did what humans are designed to do in crisis: step by step, he did the next thing to save my life. When he couldn't open a door, he attempted to break a window. When he couldn't break a window, he opened a different door. But unable to pull me from the burning truck, he seemed to be out of options.

As Matt shoved his phone back in his pocket, still pulling at me, he noticed a car coming toward us on the dark country road. It was the first sign of human life he'd seen since the crash. He would learn later that twelve-foot flames from the hood of the car had blocked his view of several cars that had stopped by the side of the road beyond the truck, and their passengers had stood outside and watched him screaming for help as he struggled to free me.

Catching that glimpse of movement, though, Matt ran about forty yards toward the road. Waving his arms to get the attention of the driver, begging him to stop and help, Matt watched helplessly as the driver slowed, looked at him, then kept driving.

Unnerved and desperate, Matt turned around and ran back toward the burning truck, reasoning with God, "I guess we're gonna have to do this alone." The glow of the blazing truck still kept Matt from seeing the growing line of spectators beyond it.

Tugging again at my wilted body, he rocked me from side to side, trying to unwedge me from the burning cab.

While Matt continued to struggle alone, the slowing car finally *did* stop by the side of the road. Jumping out of his vehicle, the driver surveyed the group of three or four people already gathered there, curious faces illumined by the glow of the fire.

The stranger, a man in his early thirties, bellowed angrily at the spectators, "Are you gonna help, or what?!"

Turning toward him, the others simply stared, remaining silent.

The stranger ran full-speed toward the truck, then stopped dead in his tracks as he and Matt both saw the same thing: my jeans were gone and the flesh of my legs was now on fire.

Fearful of coming any closer, the stranger shouted to Matt, "You have to leave him, man!"

Matt ignored him.

A second time, he instructed Matt, "You have to leave him!"

Matt kept pulling. "I'm not leaving him," he hollered back. "He's my brother!"

Matt was gripped by both adrenaline and conviction: "I'm going to get him out, or we're both going." Those were the only two outcomes he was willing to entertain.

Still aware of the peaceful angelic presence in the cab, Matt wondered impatiently if it would ever intervene.

A third time, the stranger shouted, "Get away from that truck, it's going to blow! You have to leave him! You have to leave him!"

With Matt's own burned arms still gripping my body and my blood soaking his shirt, he yelled back, "I'm not leaving him! You have to help me!"

Realizing he meant it, the stranger finally conceded. Matt grabbed my right arm, and the stranger grabbed my left. Matt counted down, "One, two, three, *pull*!"

With that, I finally fell out of the wreckage of the truck and onto the ground. The sight of me was shocking.

My battered body looked like it had been torn in half. My legs looked like they were hanging by a thread. Skin was hanging off, and they were completely charred black. The left side of my face and head were swollen and disfigured. My left cheek bone and eye socket were crushed, and my eye had popped out. Both my legs were on fire, the right from my upper thigh down to my ankle and into my Achilles tendon, the left from the top of my knee down to my lower shin and around to my calf. Both my hands were on fire and my left forearm were still smoking from the flames that had already consumed my skin. My left heel bone was fractured and my pelvis was broken.

Matt ripped off his shirt and used it along with his bare hands to beat the fire on my legs into submission. He barked at the stranger, "Help me drag him out into the field before this thing blows up!"

With each one pulling an arm, they dragged me about fifty yards from the truck into a grassy patch beside the beanfield. Fire filled the cab as the flames continued to leap fifteen feet toward the sky. Even from our safe distance, the heat from the inferno was fierce.

The stranger, who may or may not have been sober, started shouting as he ran circles around the truck.

"F***, yes!" he hollered. "We did it! Woooooo! We f***ing did it!!"

The stranger circled the beanfield bonfire three times, shouting profanities and victorious exclamations. The other onlookers continued to watch the drama unfold. The sharp smell of burning polyurethane from the interior of my truck cut through the smoky haze. And in the backseat, my beloved Takamine guitar—the one my youth pastor had played before it became mine—slowly burned.

With his eyes stinging from the smoke, Matt's vision gradually began to adjust to the darkness. He could now make out the useless roadside audience beyond the truck. Though none had come forward to help, he was confident someone would have at least called 9-1-1. Beyond the stranger's intermittent hoots and hollers punctuating the night, the roar of the fiery flames filled the night air.

Still unconscious, I quietly moaned in agony. Most of my pants had been burned away, leaving exposed flesh smoldering. It was evident that my legs and arms had been burned but there was no way to gauge my internal injuries. Matt still didn't know if I'd live or die. Putting one hand on my chest, and lifting the other to the night sky, he began praying, "Jesus, You got us this far and I know You're going to save him. You have to save him."

Suddenly, a figure emerged from deep within the lush beanfield, walking toward us through the high grass. He was wearing a button-up shirt and dark pants, gripping in his right hand the handle of a bag that hung at his side. His presence was nothing like that of the frenetic lunatic running in circles. Nor was it like that of the silent, impotent crowd. Rather, the person walked with confidence and purpose. Lit by the glowing blaze, his silhouette was crisp and clear. In the same way that a child can pick out the distinctive form of a trusted parent, or a husband can identify the outline of his bride, there was no question in Matt's mind about the identity of the person who was calmly approaching.

It was Jesus.

Help had definitely arrived.

CHAPTER 3

HELPERS

As Matt kept one hand on my chest and his singed arm raised to the heavens, the bent figure of Christ knelt down beside us, setting what appeared to be a medical bag on the grass to His side and opening it.

Tilting His head up, He looked directly into Matt's eyes, and said, "Matt, you are alright. You're going to be fine. And Mike's going to be fine."

Then He leaned over and began working on my body. He reached inside me like a mechanic might reach under a car hood and began fiddling around, occasionally pulling a useful tool from the bag. Though I wasn't physically splayed open the way someone would be during a surgical procedure at a hospital, Jesus had access to every part of my body. He worked wordlessly as Matt prayed.

Calmed by the Savior's purposeful presence, Matt finally said, "God, You are so good, God, You are so good. Jesus, You can do it. Save Mike. Save Mike."

As Matt prayed, a second figure approached. There was also no question about this man's identity: His brimmed hat and uniform signaled that he was an officer with the sheriff's department. With one glance at my burned and swollen body and hearing my low, pathetic moans, the deputy spoke into a radio on his shoulder.

"Dispatch, we're going to need a bird," he said. Then he turned to Matt. "We need to get him further away. That car's gonna blow up."

"We did that," Matt protested weakly, but helped the deputy drag me further from the blaze.

Pivoting his attention from the officer back to my body, Matt noticed that the Good Physician was no longer visible. Still running on adrenaline and too weary to process what had just happened, he again joined the officer in hooking me under my armpits and pulling me further through the thick growth of beans, doubling my distance from the truck. Then Matt dropped back down to my side, speaking words of assurance.

Within minutes an ambulance raced to the side of the road and, directed by the officer's shouts and the crowd's pointing fingers, rescuers brought a backboard to where I lay in the field. As the deputy communicated with the paramedics and his dispatcher, Matt realized that a helicopter had been canceled because it couldn't have landed in the depths of the soybean field. Instead, the ambulance would be transporting me to a clearing in a local park a few miles down the road.

As the paramedics carefully slid me onto a backboard and walked me swiftly to the waiting ambulance, flashing red lights still spinning, the deputy turned to Matt and said, "You need to come with me." They would drive together to tell my parents what had happened.

Numbly dutiful, Matt said, "My car is over there."

"Meet me at Red Bridge Park. Do you know where that is?"

The park was right across the street from Hidden Bay, the site of his family's lake house.

"Yeah," Matt said. "I'll meet you there."

He trailed the officer to Red Bridge Park, where he saw the helicopter waiting in a field adjacent to the parking lot. The inside of the ambulance was still lit up, and Matt could see it was empty because I'd already been loaded into the chopper.

"So where does his family live?" the officer asked as Matt slid into his passenger seat.

"Elderberry Road."

As the sheriff headed for our home, Matt called his mom.

"Hey Mom, Mike's been in a really serious accident and he's being life-lined down to Methodist Hospital. The sheriff and I are going to tell Mike's parents right now. I need you to meet us at their house...'kay, bye."

My parents had known Matt's folks for years through church. And they were patients at my dad's dental practice.

After a few moments of silence, the officer instructed Matt, "You'll need to tell them."

Shocked, Matt shot back, "I'm not telling them! You need to tell them."

The officer pushed back, "No, you need to tell them."

"I'm not comfortable with that," Matt protested, feeling a bit surprised to be arguing with an adult, especially a sheriff's deputy. "I really think it's better if you do it."

When they reached Elderberry Road around midnight, Matt guided the deputy to my family's home. The inside of the house looked dark, but the front porch lights were on.

As Matt walked up the sidewalk toward our front door, he glanced down and realized that he'd put on the shirt he'd used to put out the fire on my legs. Brownish bloodstains from my body had dried on it. He reeked of smoke and was blackened by soot.

The officer rang the doorbell, and my sister Rachel, who was nineteen, answered. When she saw Matt, who looked like he'd been spit out of the bowels of Hell, standing beside an officer, her face went pale.

"I'll go get Mom and Dad" was all she said.

She dashed upstairs, then quickly returned with my folks—my mom in her pajamas and my dad still dressed. Their faces already registered confusion and concern.

"Are you Mr. and Mrs. Kinney?" the deputy asked.

"Yes," my father said.

"And your son is Michael?"

"Yes," they both said, unable to hide their anxiety.

The officer coolly announced, "He's been in a serious accident. He's badly burned and is being taken to Methodist."

That concluded his presentation. (So maybe Matt *should* have told them.)

My mom, a seasoned nurse, dashed upstairs to get dressed. After the officer's swift exit my dad, stunned, lingered in the doorway.

Matt assured him, "Dr. Kinney, it's gonna be okay. Jesus was there, and it's gonna be okay."

For a moment, Matt's calm confidence convinced my dad that it *was* going to be okay. He is a man of faith, and nothing could have meant more to him in that moment than Matt's certain assurance of Christ's presence.

The bright glow of headlights cut through the darkness as Matt's parents pulled into our driveway. His mom, Joni, hurried inside to stay at our house with Rachel and my little brother John, thirteen, who was still sleeping. When my mom swept back down the stairs, Joni gave her a quick hug and sent my parents and Matt out to the waiting Chrysler minivan so Matt's dad, Jim, could drive them to Methodist Hospital. My dad got in front, and Matt sat with my mom in the back. Still high on adrenaline, he babbled words of comfort and hope for the entire twenty-minute drive, insisting that Jesus had helped me and that everything was going to be okay.

But Matt's steadfast surety wasn't going to jibe with the broken body my parents would find at the hospital.

None of my family or friends would have recognized me. My left eye hung out of its shattered socket by the optic nerve. Four of my front teeth were broken off. My swollen face was twice its normal size. Both of my lower legs were covered in third-degree burns, and the right one was completely burned from the upper thigh to the top of my foot—the fire had even seared my Achilles tendon. My left arm, both hands, and lower back were also burned. One heel was shattered.

But I was alive.

GOD IS WITH YOU

I'd lived because of an unlikely series of events that many would call "coincidence." Matt and I had not been speeding. We'd not been drinking. A rotting tree and the brush guards on my truck had dampened the brutal impact of the head-on collision. My truck had missed plowing into a concrete barrier by inches. Having so little gas in my tank when I crashed prevented an explosion. An odd, reluctant stranger helped extract me from the burning vehicle. And then there was the Good Physician, kneeling beside me, doing His work.

When there was absolutely nothing I could do to help myself, God provided a mighty quartet of helpers to rescue me. I don't take one of them for granted. Rather, I see each one as a sign of God's steadfast Presence with me.

Matt was the "expected helper." He knew me. He was my friend. He cared. But there were countless understandable reasons he could have kept a safe distance from my truck that night, starting with common sense. Fear of the truck exploding might have caused him to seek safety. He also might reasonably have figured that I was dead, or would be unlikely to survive. He might have logically calculated that there was no reason for *both* of us to die senselessly. But there was nothing common about Matt's logic. He loved me, and he trusted God. That was it. Without thinking of his own safety, he risked himself for my sake.

The "invisible helper" was the angelic presence God sent to reassure Matt. This helper wasn't extinguishing flames or bending metal, but the steadfast presence of that unseen holy one reminded Matt that he was not alone.

The reluctant guy, who we later learned was named John Kirby, was the "unexpected helper." That poor fellow was just trying to get home after being with friends and had the misfortune to drive past the site of my wreck at exactly the wrong—and by wrong I mean *right*—moment. Despite a very healthy dose of fear, this unlikely helper, like Matt, risked his own safety so I could live.

Many of those who are familiar with Jesus's story of the Good Samaritan—the man who stopped to help a hurting stranger on the side of the road—take one simple principle from it: *help others*. But too often we overlook the real scandal of Jesus's parable that would have shocked its first audience. The "hero" of the story wasn't a faithful Jew, like Jesus and His audience; he was a Samaritan who would likely have been despised both by the man he helped and by Jesus's listeners. Jesus was lauding the sacrifice of the "unexpected helper." That was John Kirby.

And the final aide God provided, the one I'll call the "reliable helper," was the Person of Jesus. In ways that I will never understand, He showed himself to be faithful and present with Matt as He gently began to knit my body back together. The person of Jesus we meet in the gospels is the same Person who showed up to care for me.

When we endure fiery trials in our lives, it's natural to wonder if God is with us and for us in our suffering. Of course we wonder. We desperately want to believe that God was near—that God *is* near—but a quiet part of us fears that in our darkest moment we are alone. And our *feelings*—of anxiety, sadness, anger, and confusion—bully us. Echoing the voice of the enemy, our feelings hiss that God is not present. God is not good. God cannot be trusted.

And yet as God's gracious Spirit opens the eyes of our hearts, we begin to notice the ways He has been present in our suffering. He provides "expected" helpers, like Matt. They stick by us, like brothers, like sisters, in our most terrifying moments. And like the "invisible" angelic presence in my truck, God is present with us spiritually in ways we might not even understand. God also shows up through "unexpected" aides like John Kirby. Maybe an acquaintance says just the right word to you at just the right time. Or an unlikely stranger might pause to offer assistance when you need it most. And sometimes we have the privilege of witnessing the steadfast, faithful presence of the "reliable" Helper who is Jesus. Matt got to see Him with his eyes. And, after that night, I would grow to see Him clearly with the eyes of my heart.

Beloved, a gracious God longs to make His presence known to you through the person of Jesus. It's what He did a few thousand years ago in coming to be with us in the flesh and it's what He does today.

I would need more divine intervention in the weeks and months ahead.

CHAPTER 4

THE UNKNOWN

When my parents arrived at the hospital, I was having a CT scan, so they had to wait for two hours to see me. I'd been put into a drug-induced coma to keep me still for the first several days after my accident. Throughout the night, family and friends flooded into the emergency room, then were directed to the conference room where my parents were waiting.

Although the nurses had washed much of the blood covering my body away by the time my folks were finally invited into the room where I was being treated, nothing could disguise my grossly swollen head and burned body. They spent a few moments speaking to me even though I was unconscious, comforting and loving me, before a nurse asked them to leave so they could get some X-rays.

My mother beelined to the waiting area that was filled with family and friends to update them. Small groups of teens and families were huddled in chairs and against walls praying for me but quieted down to receive her report. In those earliest hours, unfortunately, she wasn't able to offer more than, "We don't know yet."

Meanwhile, my father pivoted down an empty hall to find a quieter space. Noticing an empty gurney parked there, he hopped on it to sit down and rest. He buried his head in his hands, and then my hero and the rock of our family began to weep.

As my mom's friends reached out to comfort her, a few of my father's friends hunted him down to find him sobbing alone. What weighed on him most heavily in that moment was that neither his great love for me nor even his own medical training could spare me from what I'd experienced and would continue to endure. The grim reality was more than he could bear.

My mom reacted differently. She would tell you that from the moment she saw me, she went into "nurse mode." Whenever a medical professional would update her, she'd deliver her report to the rest of the family like the consummate professional she was. She also remembers having a keen sense of peace while she was surrounded by the army of praying friends.

Until I was awake, doctors would have no way to know the extent of my brain injury, nor whether or how my burned and broken body would recover. During those long hours of watching and waiting, my parents prayed mightily day and night, begging God to spare my life and restore my health.

My friend Jason, who came to the hospital that night, says today that seeing my head swollen to the size of a basketball was pretty terrifying. In the hours after the accident, my face and head had blown up to double their usual size. I'd also been fitted with a

C-collar, which is basically a bulky neck brace, to protect my neck and spine until I was fully alert. I looked very little like the kid who'd dozed off in history class the previous day.

After I was transported to a room in the ICU, nurses inserted clear plastic breathing tubes into my nostrils and secured them with white medical tape. The 30 percent of my body that had been burned was now covered by skin thinner than paper, so frail that the slightest movement could tear it, increasing the risk of infection. Three limbs were wrapped and rewrapped daily as those burns healed. But as they improved, they itched. It would have been pretty hard to resist scratching if I had been in my right mind, which I definitely was not. During those first weeks nurses frequently had to tie my hands to the bedrails to keep me from touching my skin.

Meanwhile, my restless legs kept moving. Eventually, that movement wore a hole in the back of my heel, a wound that would slowly expand to the diameter of a water bottle. The stiller I could remain in bed, the better the chance my skin would have to heal. But lying still was nearly impossible.

Two days after my accident, I had surgery to graft healthy skin harvested from my waist to one of the burned areas on my leg where the fire had completely decimated my skin. To my parents' relief, that first surgery went well. There would be several more to come.

The next day, my dad returned to his dental practice while my mom stayed at my bedside, praying and gently holding my hand. Just as a host of God-sent helpers arrived during the accident, one was now in my hospital room. Every day my mother kept vigilant watch like a fierce mama bear protecting her cub. As nurses decreased my sedatives and I slowly began to regain consciousness,

I squeezed my mom's hand. So when my dad came by the hospital after seeing patients all day, she was excited for him to experience my new level of alertness.

"Here, Wayne, hold his hand," she directed as he slid into the chair beside my bed.

"Hey buddy, I'm glad to see you," he said.

Using her thumb and forefinger, my mom held my right eye open. In response to his words, I looked at him and weakly squeezed his hand.

I saw my dad's eyes fly open wide, then look to my mom for confirmation as he realized I was back, if only in a small way. Flooded with relief, he released the fear I would remain in a vegetative state that had been gripping him. That little squeeze filled him with new hope.

On my fifth day in pediatric ICU, my nurses took me off one sedative and cut the second one in half. After that, I began to grow restless and started waking up more often.

There was a small CD player next to my bed. One of the songs my mom kept on repeat was Caedmon's Call's "Before There Was Time," which describes the God who counts the hairs on our head and knows every word that passes our lips. The lyrics that resonated in my heart were, "You saved me, You pulled me from the grave." And the response to God's rescue is to praise the One who saves. As I slowly began to return to life mentally, it was the response of my heart in that season. *I'd* been saved. *I'd* been pulled from the grave.

Matt came to visit me that first week while I was still pretty groggy. I emerged from sleep to see him standing beside my bed as my mother prayed. She says I was trying to cry, but no sound would come out.

"Mom?" I asked as I struggled toward wakefulness.

She reached over to turn down Caedmon's Call.

"I'm right here," she assured me, "and Matt's here, too."

I said, "I wanna see Matt."

"Hey bro," Matt said. "I'm right here."

I was too altered to notice the fear in his voice. Pauses in our communication were a bit longer than usual as my brain wrestled to arrange words into coherent sentences.

Pointing to my breathing tube, I proudly announced, "I got a noodle in my nose!"

Smiling, Matt kindly confirmed, "Yeah, you do."

I wrestled to choose the right words. "Matt," I finally asked, "what's up? What's going on, man?"

Fighting to sound normal, Matt choked out, "Well, I'm trying. I'm in classes, trying to do my work…"

At that time, I couldn't have begun to imagine the kind of emotional turmoil he had been experiencing and would continue to endure.

"So," I asked, "is everything okay?"

"What do you mean?" he asked.

"The accident," I explained, as if my awkward query should be as plain as day.

"Well, Mike," he said slowly, choosing his words carefully, "it was a pretty bad accident."

"Just tell me," I insisted.

My mom had explained to Matt that I was a little out of it. Although he was haunted by very clear memories of that night, he didn't yet know what I remembered. No one did.

"What do you remember?" he asked gently.

I closed my eyes and returned to the evening of Friday, August 16.

"I remember going to the football game," I reported.

"Yeah," he concurred, "and then we went to O'Charley's..."

I smiled as I thought about talking with the cute girls.

Though I'd not retain all of it, and would need to ask him again on other occasions, Matt proceeded to describe all that he remembered of that night. In his voice I heard faint echoes of the terror he endured. But when he got to the part of the story after I'd been extricated from the car, his voice gained energy and momentum.

"Mike, Jesus was there!" he exclaimed, his face lighting up.

"Wait, what?" I asked. As the church kid who had been pursuing my own walk of faith, I'd been assured that God is with us, even in hard times. And this sounded a lot like that.

"Mike," he continued, his voice picking up volume and speed, "He had this black doctor's bag. And I was kneeling across from Him, beside you, as He was healing you."

I'd heard of modern-day people in various crises encountering Jesus, but had never dreamed I'd be one of them. It was more than I could digest.

"I'd prayed, asking Him to help us. Begging. I asked for Him to come, and He came!"

I knew I wasn't at my sharpest, and I had to make sure I was tracking. "You mean He was there?!"

"Yeah," Matt confirmed, wide-eyed and nodding. "*He was there.*"

This was powerful. Matt and I had shared an encounter with God that few people would ever experience. The local news outlets were hailing Matt as a local hero, but I'd later learn that he didn't feel like one. He felt traumatized. Though he was a pretty determined guy, Matt was wrestling just to complete his homework. At school, he might burst into tears in the hallway. While my body had borne the physical brunt of the accident, Matt had carried the emotional weight of it. Over the following months, he would begin to spread out his visits to me, as they were so emotionally taxing for him.

Matt was convinced that the only Person who deserved credit for saving my life was Jesus. And even though I hadn't seen Him with my physical eyes, that image—of Jesus showing up to care for me—is one that has been seared into the deepest places of my mind and heart.

The night I was admitted to the hospital, nobody knew if I would live or die. They didn't know if I'd be in a permanent vegetative state. They didn't know if I'd walk. They didn't know if I'd be horribly scarred. All any of us could do was take one day at a time. One hour at a time. One moment at a time.

But while I was incapacitated, my mother was exhausted, my father was terrified, Matt was traumatized, and my siblings were neglected, there was an army of supporters helping to sustain us. Countless friends from church and school and the neighborhood flooded the emergency room on the night of my accident. Hundreds more from Northview lifted us up in prayer. A friend of my mom's coordinated my little brother's transportation to and from school and other events. Another friend organized a rotating caravan of meals that arrived on our front porch nightly. Cards and letters, inked with care and prayer, flooded our mailbox. The members of our community poured themselves out on our behalf in immeasurably creative ways.

And in every prayer, every green bean casserole, every card, my family and I experienced the steadfast care of the One who was with us and for us.

CHAPTER 5

A LITTLE LOOPY

*M*y *truck is on fire, and I have to get out!*

Legs burning, I wrestled to get out of the blazing inferno. Weakened, paralyzed, I pushed at my legs, willing them to move. One thought consumed me: *I've got to get out.*

I knew that if I didn't get out of the truck, I'd be burned alive.

"Help!"

Why isn't anyone helping me get out of this truck?

Louder, I yelled, "Somebody help me!"

In the next moment, my mom was at my side. But instead of pulling me out, she was holding me in.

"I've got to get out! The truck is going to blow up," I insisted.

"Mike," she said calmly in her nurse voice, "it's not safe. You need to stay in bed. What do you need?"

I felt desperate.

"I'm on fire!!!" I yelled. "Let me out!"

If I could just drag myself out of here...

My mom's eyes darted toward the door to the hallway.

Spotting my nurse, Terry, she called out, "Could I get some help, please?!"

Terry rushed in. "Mike, you're in the hospital," she said. "You're safe. You're not on fire."

What is wrong with them? Why aren't these people helping me get out?!

I groggily began to notice my surroundings. I was in a bed. It looked like a hospital room. Most of my body was bandaged.

Slowly I began to piece together bits of reality.

"Oh, wait, am I in a hospital?"

Terry repeated, "Yes, you are. You're safe. And we're taking good care of you."

Seeing another woman at her side, I asked, "And who are you?"

With an amused smile, the woman who'd given me life gently replied, "I'm your mom."

Dubious, I pressed, "Are you really my mom?"

"Yes," she assured me.

"Sweet."

For a moment, I was satisfied. But only a moment.

"But where's Dad?" I demanded.

Mom gently answered, "He's at work, Mike. You'll see him later."

Growing agitated again, I asked, "But how far away is he? How long will it take him to get here? Why isn't he here? Is an ambulance coming?"

Calmly, Mom kept trying to orient me to reality. "Mike, you're in the hospital, and you're safe."

"No!" I barked. "I can't stay here. It's not safe. I've got to get out of here. Why aren't you helping me?"

My mom looked at Terry to signal that she needed more help.

"Hang on, Mike," Terry said, gently touching my arm with her fingertips. "Let me get you something."

When Terry dipped out into the hallway, Mom began telling me what each of my family members was doing that day. Dad was seeing patients. My brother, John, who had a broken arm, was at school, and when classes were over, he'd watch his team's football practice. Rachel, who'd called that morning to check on me, was going to class. While I was still restless and agitated, my mom's voice was soothing.

When Terry returned, I got wound up again. Thinking she had come to assist with my rescue from the burning truck, I began trying to fight my way out of bed again. While Mom held each arm, Terry wrapped a restraint around each of my wrists, securing them to the bedrails. When I was restrained, she inserted an IV in one of them and quietly murmured, "Two milligrams of Ativan."

"Mike," Mom said soothingly, "this medicine is going to help you feel better. So close your eyes and relax. I'm here. Terry's here. And we're going to take care of you, honey."

Though my insides were still screaming "fight" and "flight," I began to relax. When I finally drifted off to sleep again, Mom collapsed into her chair, where she continued to keep watch over her unglued child.

Later that afternoon, my friend Scott showed up for a visit.

"Hey dude," he called out as he approached my bed.

Recognizing him, and glad for the visit, I answered, "Hey man, good to see you."

Whatever small talk that took place next must have signaled to him that I wasn't all there.

Gently, Scott asked, "Do you remember what happened, Mike?"

I was pretty sure I did. "I think I fell down some stairs."

Scott couldn't conceal his delight at what was my best guess. Then he gently explained that I'd been in a car accident a week earlier.

"Who does that?!" I asked with a hint of outrage. Meaning, "Who crashes their car for no reason?" Something about it did sound familiar, though, and I started getting more and more riled up. Soon I was yelling at the top of my lungs.

"Help! Help! Somebody help me!"

Scared by my outburst, Scott stepped back and let my mom step in.

"Mike," she said in a hushed voice, "stop yelling or you'll wake the babies."

I was one of the oldest patients in the pediatric ICU; some were newborns. We'd often seen parents walking the halls holding them.

"Screw the babies!" I shouted. "Throw them off the ship!"

It was not one of my finer moments.

When Dad got off work that evening, he came straight to the hospital to give Mom a break. She kissed my forehead and went home to heat up dinner for John and get some rest. Once there, she was greeted by the fresh scent of a lemony household cleaning product. A big bouquet of flowers was on the kitchen table, and a fresh stack of cards had arrived in the mail; among them she found a note from a group of her friends. They'd cleaned the entire house and left a plate of freshly baked chocolate-chip cookies.

That was when she finally wept for her oldest son. She dropped onto a kitchen chair and finally let her guard down, ditched her "nurse mom" role, and released all the emotion that had been building inside. As the person who'd been my round-the-clock caregiver for days, somehow the care she'd received from her friends had made room for her to finally just *be*.

Although I didn't like it, I was beginning to get used to my hospital life and was even starting to know what to expect. Discomfort, from mild to severe, was par for the course.

In the hospital, I always felt thirsty. It seemed counterintuitive to me that I was being denied fluids, since water is supposed to be good for you. Even though those of us on the swim team were surrounded by water, we still needed to stay hydrated to perform at the highest level, just like any other athletes. So when I was swimming, I consumed a lot of Gatorade, and yellow was my color/flavor of choice.

But Mom had explained to me that I couldn't drink water because if I suddenly needed an emergency procedure, like surgery, where anesthesia was required, having anything in my stomach—including water—increased my risk of vomiting or aspirating. Also, anesthesia suppresses the body's natural gag reflex, and this can lead to all kinds of bad things if you're aspirating.

Thankfully I *was* allowed to have ice chips. I guess the logic there is that it just helps patients consume way *less* water than drinking it. The hospital had pellet-shaped ice chips; I called them "miracle ice," since any kind of hydration in my mouth felt miraculous. (Clearly, my "miracle" bar was pretty low.)

Many nights I dreamed that a big truck came to my hospital room and a delivery guy would fill my room with pallets of Gatorade—orange, yellow, blue, red. I would stretch and strain as hard as I could to reach them from my bed, but always failed. When I woke up, I'd be desperately thirsty.

But thirst and chills and sweats were the *minor* inconveniences of hospital life. I also experienced brutal withdrawal symptoms when doctors weaned me off some of the opioid painkillers my body had needed in the weeks after the accident. My muscles were achy, I had trouble sleeping, and I felt anxious and restless. Because I'd tried to get out of bed unauthorized—sometimes aggressively—the staff had hung a soccer net around my bed to cage me in. My amazing nurses worked tirelessly on my behalf to ensure that I wouldn't hurt myself.

I would later learn that some of the ridiculous things I said when I was doped up became my family's favorite dinnertime entertainment during the few meals they were able to share during my hospitalization. Some—like what I'd shouted about throwing babies off ships—were pure lunacy. But other things I'd said in altered states that were less likely to stem from drugs were scarier. The dream I had about being trapped in my truck was particularly telling. While my mind was not conscious in the aftermath of the crash, my body remembered. I'd stored the terror in my cells, and in my slumber, my insides were trying to work it all out. When I rested, my deep places were trying to make sense of what had happened.

THE GIFT OF WEAKNESS

Suffering makes us keenly aware of our vulnerability. One hour I was a healthy student athlete who had the world by the tail—and in the next hour, my life was hanging by a thread. When we suffer, we face the reality of our own mortality. We might not be *thinking* about death when calamity befalls us, but when we suffer we are forced to face its nearness while we live in these earthly bodies. An unexpected diagnosis screams that we are vulnerable. A physical or intellectual disability hisses whispers of our fragility. Perhaps an unplanned pregnancy suddenly causes a woman to fear she will not be able to feed herself or her child. When we encounter unexpected challenges we are forced to face the fact that although we are living, the forces of sin and death in this world are present and strong.

Since the night of my accident I've become more keenly aware of the fragility of life, both mine and others'. My family has as well. And something about facing that reality squarely seems more real, more *right*, than clinging to the daily conviction that we are invincible. We're not. Whether or not we admit it, we are vulnerable. But in every moment there is One who sees us, who hears us, who knows us, who loves us. And in the weeks after my accident, that fact became more real to my family and me *because* we were in need.

The sing-song children's classic "Jesus Loves Me" reminds us, "We are weak but He is strong." If you are weak today, or if there was a season of your life when you were particularly vulnerable, know there is a gift in seeing your vulnerability squarely for what it is. Weakness creates a unique space for you to recognize the ways that Jesus is strong on your behalf.

When Mom returned to the hospital the day after Scott's visit, I wasn't a lot more coherent than I'd been when she'd last seen me. As soon as she arrived, one of my nurses, Cassie, pulled her aside.

"Lois," she said, "he was disoriented again this morning."

Mom's face fell, knowing how belligerent I could become.

"When I asked him where he was," Cassie continued, "he insisted he was at home. When I asked Mike who I was, he said 'Rachel.'"

Mom smiled.

Cassie continued, "So I asked, 'Am I your sister?' And he said, 'Unfortunately.'"

While that ugly little exchange might have disappointed another mom, mine was delighted. That my imaginary interaction was so normal somehow comforted her.

Mom slipped into my room, pulled her Bible and journal out of her canvas tote, and opened up to a passage she'd been meditating on. In Paul's letter to the believers in Ephesus, he wrote that he'd prayed for the people he loved the way my mom had been praying for me. That day she'd paused to camp out on his final sentences: "Now to him who is able to do immeasurably more than all we ask or imagine, according to his power that is at work within us, to him be glory in the church and in Christ Jesus throughout all generations, for ever and ever! Amen" (Ephesians 3:20–21).

Him who is able to do immeasurably more than all we ask or imagine. That mighty One was the God to whom she was praying! Of course she'd asked God to save my life and to mend my body. And she was coming to discover God, and call on Him, as the One who goes above and beyond, doing more than we can comprehend.

She'd read the Scripture silently several times, and had paused to meditate on what God wanted to teach her that day, when she heard my voice.

"This is my life, I give it all to you…"

I was singing.

She couldn't help smiling, especially in the wake of my traumatic awakening the previous morning.

When I'd finished singing the comforting song of praise, I continued on as if I was speaking into a microphone leading worship in the Barn, the building where my youth group met every Sunday night.

"God," I began praying in a stage voice, believing I was leading my peers, "You are holy. And when You fill our hearts, we are never the same. Father, we offer our lives to You, because You are worthy. Take our lives and use them for Your glory. We ask in the name of Jesus."

While that should have been the end of my hospital prayer, I continued, "You can all take a seat now, and we're going to hear a message from Don tonight."

When I slowly returned to full consciousness, Mom was wearing a big smile on her face. My moving "performance" had reminded her of the guy I was before my accident.

CHAPTER 6

THE GUY I HAD BEEN

One Sunday afternoon when I was in seventh grade, our whole family had shown up at church a few hours before youth group to paint the building in which the youth met. "The Barn" had been white when it was built, and on that day, we were painting it red.

As I dragged a ragged paint brush along the bottom of the building, painting the edges near the grass, I heard music coming from the auditorium inside. Setting my paintbrush down, I wiped my hands on the grass and went inside to see what was up. On stage, I saw high school kids about Rachel's age who were having some kind of rehearsal. A few were strumming guitars. One sat behind a set of drums. Another gripped a microphone stand as he sang. As I listened in, I figured out that they were preparing to lead the high school youth group in worship. We did the same in our middle school youth group, but the band consisted of college-aged kids and adult leaders. In that moment, seeing kids who were just a few years older than me ignited something in my heart that continues to burn to this day.

After listening for a while, I hurried outside to find my parents painting the back of the Barn with rollers.

"Hey," I began, "I *really* want to play the guitar. Can I get a guitar?"

"Slow down, buddy," my dad said. "I don't want you to *start* with guitar—"

"Who's *starting* music?" I protested. "I can play the *piano*."

"I know, Mike," he said patiently, "but if you're going to take up a stringed instrument, I want you to get some experience on the violin first."

"Violin?!" I protested. "What good is a violin?"

"You'll learn the basics," he explained, "and after you play for a year we'll talk about a guitar."

While other kids I knew would lobby and whine and cajole, I could hear in my dad's voice that his mind was made up. So in eighth grade, I did my due diligence by playing violin at school. I was committed to it, too, because, for me, it was the gateway instrument that would give me access to the guitar.

By my thirteenth birthday, I'd earned my way there, and my dad gave me a handmade Arts & Lutherie guitar. I began by strumming it in my room, picking at strings, and realized I needed to learn chords, so I bought a book about chords at Guitar Center. When I would press my fingers against the frets of the guitar in my bedroom, I imagined that I was leading worship for the youth in the Barn. It's what had gotten me through violin, and it's what would drive me to improve until I was ready for the big show.

In a lot of ways, Northview Church was a hub of our family's life together. My dad was serving as an elder and my mom was active in the church's ministry. And because my dad was known by many in the congregation, to a lot of them I wasn't "Mike"; I was "Wayne Kinney's son." And that was OK with me. Though I wasn't technically a pastor's kid, my siblings and I were part of a tribe who arrived at church events a little earlier than other families and left a little later because of our parents' involvement. The family with whom we shared life most deeply were the Sorums. If families had other "best friend" families, this was ours. Pat Sorum's husband, Jim, had been an associate pastor at Northview, and the three Sorum kids—Jamie, Micah, and Jacob—matched up in age pretty closely with me and my two siblings. Age-wise, Jamie was between Rachel and me. Micah, a girl, was a grade below me, though just a few months younger. And Jacob and John were the same age. Basically, we were a litter of church kids who shared a lot of life together. We celebrated Easter together. We played hide-and-seek at the church. We had sleepovers at one another's homes. We traveled together every year to Destin, Florida, where we shared a condo. One year we even went to Disney World!

When Rachel drove me to my first day of youth group as a high school freshman, I noticed my friend Jamie Sorum was in the mix of almost two hundred kids who'd gathered on a Sunday night in early September.

"Hey, Jamie!" I said as we were heading into service. "Can I sit with you?"

"Of course!" she said, "Follow me! I'll show you where I usually sit."

I was hoping it was close to the stage because I had been looking forward to seeing the worship band play up close. They were starting to play as we made our way to the seats.

"Thanks for letting me sit with you!" I said.

Jamie laughed. "Of course, Mike!"

I was transfixed as I watched Don lead the worship band, just as I had been two years earlier. His eyes were closed as he strummed his guitar and swayed gently as he led. What I thought I noticed in his posture, which I surely couldn't have articulated at the time, was someone who wasn't as much interested in winning the attention of others as he was concerned about directing our attention to God.

After the first song, "God of Wonders," he prayed aloud, "Lord, we're here for You. This is not about us, it's about who You are. We invite You to be in this place with us today."

For the record, if you've ever met a teenager, it kind of usually *is* about them. But he gently tipped the eyes of our hearts away from ourselves, away from our peers, away from the band, and toward the Father who loved us and wanted to meet us.

The second week of youth group, I asked Rachel to drive us early so that I could talk to Don. He was wrapping up band rehearsal and students were just starting to trickle into the auditorium.

"Don?" I asked as he rearranged the pages on his music stand. "I really feel like I want to get involved with the worship team. Do you think I could do this?"

Smiling, he offered, "Well, I need to hear you play. So let's have you come in for an audition. Can you stop by and see me Wednesday after school?"

"Yes!" I announced, probably a little too loudly.

"Great!" he answered. "I'll see you then."

I decided I wanted to play "Here is My Life Lord, I Give it to You" for Don. After youth group that night I went home and started practicing. And practicing. And then practicing some more. By Wednesday, every person who lived in my home would likely have been happy for the Lord to take my life, if only so they didn't have to hear the song anymore.

My performance for Don after school on Wednesday wasn't winning any Grammys, but it went as well as it could have. I nailed the melody, though my rhythm was slightly off. My fingers missed a few strings, causing the chords to sound incomplete. My voice was strong. I desperately hoped he'd let me join.

"Great job, Mike," Don said when I finished. "I think you'll do great on the team."

Relief washed over me at the sound of those words.

He continued, "We'll have you start by singing, and when you're ready I'll invite you to play the guitar."

"Awesome," I said, "that sounds so great."

Looking more serious, he said, "We take rehearsal pretty seriously. So I expect to see you every week. If that's not going to work for you, it might not be a fit, but if you can make it a priority, we'd love to have you."

"I can," I promised. "I can."

"I'm glad to hear it, Mike. Next week I want you to be here at four and we'll run through the set together."

"I'm in, I'm in! I'll be here."

When I showed up the next week, I was fired up to practice with the band. Music stands had been set up on the stage and a girl was passing out pages with the song lyrics and the corresponding chords above each word.

Walking over to where Don was unrolling cords, I asked, "Should I just sing?"

He turned to see me gripping my guitar case.

"Well," he offered, "why don't you practice both guitar and vocals today, but for the service you'll just sing. Sound good?"

"Yup," I said, "sounds good."

I asked another student where I should set up, and she pointed to a seat beside one of the music stands. When we launched into the set, I realized that I already knew the most common chords. But as the rest of the team rolled smoothly through rehearsal, I was struggling to hit one particular chord. Feeling embarrassed and frustrated, I looked toward Don to read his reaction.

"Mike, don't worry about it," he said. "You're doing great."

Through his words and actions, Don consistently communicated that he believed in me.

My first set with the band wasn't the first time I'd performed for an audience. At Stony Creek Elementary School as a second grader, I'd had a star role in the Christmas program singing "Silent Night" in the middle of the school gymnasium. The experience of soloing had whet my appetite to continue performing. As a result, I joined the Indianapolis Children's Choir, where I'd audition for solos and feel affirmed when I got them. That's where I discovered that when I heard a tune, I could learn to repeat the lyrics and melody after a time or two, which I learned not everyone can do.

Don's confidence in my abilities—founded initially on nothing other than my *desire* to lead worship—taught me to believe in myself. I'd seen Don giving others hope through music and I wanted to do it as well. I'd seen my parents serving at the church—teaching classes, leading marriage workshops, serving as leaders—and I was eager to find my place as a servant of Jesus.

At the end of my sophomore year, when Don was prepping his sermon, he called me to ask if I'd lead worship the following Sunday.

"Wait," I clarified. "You mean *lead* lead? Like you lead?"

"Well," he said, "I'll be there, but I'd like to turn things over to you and invite you to lead the group."

His confidence blew me away. And because Don was a great worship leader, I began to have confidence that *I* could be a strong leader, too.

In that season when I was leading the worship team, I was also doing life with a life group of guys who knew me and loved me. Jason, whose dad was the church's mission pastor, was part of that tribe of church staff kids. John was pretty chill and laid back. Sam, who was also a part of Northview's worship band, was *hysterical*. Matt was the high achiever of the group with his eyes set on med school. We'd meet on Thursday nights and bring our lives before each other and God, earnestly seeking whatever He had in store for us.

During Sunday morning worship, the five of us were hearing what every other adult member of Northview heard: "You were made for a purpose. God has a purpose for your life." Although it wasn't clear to me what that purpose might be, a lot of people in my community thought they *did* know what I was made for.

After leading worship for a season, adult youth group volunteers would encourage me by saying, "You have a gift. There's obviously a calling on your life." Starry-eyed students who listened to Christian music throughout the week would say, "You have such a great voice! You're going to do what Michael W. Smith does. You're going to be the next Chris Tomlin." At the time, Michael W. Smith's songs were topping the Christian charts. Because my middle initial is "W," a lot of kids in the youth group liked to call me "Michael W." Chris Tomlin, on the other hand, had made a name for himself as a worship leader. I was flattered by the comparisons, and the constant chorus of generous affirmation did make me consider whether my purpose might be tied up in music.

By the end of my junior year, well-meaning family friends began to ask, "So what do you think you'll do after graduation?" I'd been raised in a home where it was always assumed I'd go to college, and I never questioned that. I'd looked at Liberty University in Virginia and was also considering a few other schools. But of course, the "What will you do?" question and its sibling "Where will you go?" were always laden with expectation. What will you *do* for God? Where will you *go* for God? Like a lot of kids my age, I was wondering, "What am I *supposed* to do?"

And there it was.

Kids at school who weren't trying to follow God were being asked the same questions about colleges and vocation. And their answers usually came down to announcing what they might study that matched their interests and gifts. But when friends' parents asked me what I saw for my future, I understood there was an inherent expectation in that question. The expectation was the tacit agreement between us that God had a plan for my life. God had something specific for Mike Kinney to do. And while I would have loved to tell those caring and curious adults that I'd been visited by a future-telling angel—who'd offered a divine announcement of my intended institution of higher learning, the major I'd pursue there, a prestigious internship upon college graduation, and a very clear career path after that—I could boast of no such thing. Instead, I was like most of my other friends from church: I wanted to do whatever God wanted me to do; I just had no idea what that might be.

While I tried to act humble about it, I secretly hoped that those who were predicting I'd lead packed stadiums of worshipers were right. And on the morning in the hospital, when my mom caught me waking from sleep in a state of leading a crowd in praising God, it looked like they might be.

CHAPTER 7

"WE MIGHT HAVE TO TAKE THE LEG"

"The right leg is what's troubling me," the surgeon reported to my father. "We attempted to repair the vessels, but we're not getting a good blood flow. We're treating an infection there now, and I'm very concerned. I think we might have to take the leg."

It was the possibility my parents had most feared.

Ten days after the accident, when my fever had gone down and I was a bit more stable, I had surgery to repair my messed-up face. Entering through my eye and lip, doctors reconstructed my shattered eye socket, implanting screws to hold my bones together.

Immediately afterward, a new team of doctors tackled my legs. The surgery began at 11:15 at night! Because the fire had burned through the flesh on my right leg down to the bone, there wasn't a lot to work with. The damage to my lower leg, destroying the blood cells that fight infection, was pretty severe. In order to graft skin harvested from my middle and upper thigh to the burned flesh, there needed to be a blood supply, but doctors weren't able to get blood to flow to the most damaged areas. The graft wasn't successful, and they were concerned about the possibility of infection—which could be deadly.

After four hours of surgery, the doctor, covered in my blood, emerged from the operating room to speak to my parents during the wee hours of the morning. Pulling off his face mask and removing his surgical rubber gloves, Dr. Harris delivered his assessment.

Knowing my parents had medical training, he cut to the chase, "The left leg and hand look good. The grafts were successful."

My mom squeezed my dad's hand, celebrating the good news. But the concern on Dr. Harris's face signaled that there was more news to come that wasn't as good—and that concerned the failed graft on my right leg and the looming specter of amputation.

Without missing a beat, Dad answered, "No."

He understood *why* this was the recommendation. He knew that amputating my leg could save my life by protecting me from a deadly infection. But he wasn't having it.

Dr. Harris began to explain, "The risk of that lower leg getting infected—"

Dad interjected, firmly, "No, we're going to wait a couple days. I want to get a second opinion on it."

"Alright," Dr. Harris conceded, "we'll be keeping an eye on the infection."

My mom finally spoke. "Doctor, thank you so much for your work tonight. We're so grateful."

Extending his hand to Dr. Harris, Dad added, "Yes, thank you."

After the doctor left, Mom turned to him and asked, "Are you sure?"

"I'm sure we're going to try," he said.

After surgery, I was wheeled back into my hospital room. Though she hadn't slept a wink that night, Mom assumed her post by my bedside. Though I wasn't fully awake, the next morning, I roused enough to hear her calling in the troops to pray. Just a few phone calls unleashed an army of prayer warriors who would be praying ceaselessly for the healing of my legs.

By noon I was finally regaining consciousness.

Curious, my first words were, "How did the surgery go?"

"The left leg and hand went great," Mom said, "but there's still some more work to do on your right leg."

Somehow, in that moment I knew exactly where I was and why I was there.

I hesitantly asked, "Mom…?"

"What is it, honey?" she asked, leaning in.

Not wanting to say the words out loud, I choked out, "Am I going to die?"

More than anything I wanted to see her face soften, and then light up, quickly reassuring me without reservation that I'd be fine. But that's not what I saw. Deliberately, she told me the truth.

"In time you're going to be fine," she said cautiously. "But we really don't know about your legs."

I wasn't sure exactly what she meant, but didn't want to ask.

She continued, "The doctors just aren't sure right now. You might end up using a wheelchair, but we just don't know."

In retrospect, I think "using a wheelchair" was a pretty classy way to preface a possible amputation. In that moment, the prospect terrified me.

"Mike," Mom said looking me directly in the eye, "we're going to take this one day at a time. There are a lot of people praying for you and we're trusting that God is a good healer."

I nodded my head, processing what she'd said and what she hadn't said.

"Dad and I have been praying, the church has been praying, and people we don't even know have been praying. Mike, even though we can't yet see everything, we know God has got this."

Her faith buoyed my own.

At every turn, my family was seeing God's gracious hand. I began to recount the ways.

First, at the accident site, I veered off the right side of the road and over an embankment, plowing through a hollow tree that helped to slow my speed.

Then my truck veered back toward the road and across it. Unconscious, barreling out of control, I nearly missed an immovable concrete pole before my truck finally slammed into a telephone pole.

Because I was broke, the gas tank was close to empty of fuel that otherwise would have fed an explosion.

Matt bravely stepped up to do what countless onlookers would not.

An angelic presence arrived to comfort and inspire.

When Matt begged the heavens for assistance, one motorist stopped to help, risking his own safety.

And then there was Jesus.

The miraculous mysteries would only keep coming as my treatment continued.

Signs of God's saving power were abundantly plain to my family in those early days. And those countless moments of grace—the ones we could see and the ones we could not—continued to convince us that God's mighty hand had preserved my life and was continuing to heal me.

The truth was that my parents didn't know if I would keep my leg. But they did have a direct line to the Good Physician in whose care I was held.

Hours after my surgery, a friend gave my dad the number of a Dr. Jones who specialized in plastic surgery. While mine wasn't the kind of case this doctor would typically take, my father begged him for his help. Persuaded, Dr. Jones agreed to try.

Because time was of the essence, the very next day, at 11:30 a.m., I was put under anesthesia again and wheeled into surgery with Dr. Jones. My parents settled in to the waiting room to pray and wait for word.

But just fifteen minutes after beginning the surgery, Dr. Jones appeared in the doorway of the waiting room. Concerned and surprised, my parents jumped up to meet him.

"Wayne," he said to my dad, "it doesn't look nearly as bad as I'd feared. In fact, I know we can do this. Just wanted to keep you looped in."

Suddenly emotional, "Thank you" was all my father could choke out before Dr. Jones returned to the operating room.

Just thirty-two hours earlier, my parents had stood in the exact same spot and been told that I'd likely lose my leg. Flooded with relief, each knew that the change in my leg had been no less than a miraculous gift from God in response to the prayers of His people.

"Wayne," my mom said, "I don't think I told you that Pauline called last night."

Pauline was one of my mom's dear friends.

"And?" he asked, curious.

"She's reading a book by Francine Rivers, and there's a story about two doctors discussing a young patient who'd been left for dead. One of the doctors was preparing to amputate her right leg, but when he went to perform the surgery, the leg looked great. After the surgery, the girl told the doctor that Jesus had healed her."

"Well," he said, "that does sound like our God."

When my surgery ended mid-afternoon, Dr. Jones confirmed that it had been a success. While the grafts would take time to fully heal, he was confident that I'd have full use of my leg.

When I was transported back to recovery, nurses kept me asleep. Knowing that both my siblings were at the house and that I'd remain unconscious, my parents agreed to go home for dinner. Before they left, they prayed over me, thanking God for the gift of His healing. And while they were grateful for Dr. Jones, they knew who my Healer was.

After six additional surgeries, the work of His helpers was done.

At seventeen, I was noticing how my parents responded to a life-altering trauma. I'd seen their faith in action at church, on mission trips, and in our community, but I hadn't yet seen them face a challenge like this one. And I was seeing that the God they thanked and praised in good times was the One they turned to and on whom they relied in bad times. But it wasn't just my parents. I was surrounded by a beautiful tribe of believers who were counting on God to heal my body and my brain. So as a teenager, I had a unique opportunity to see faith in action when it was needed most.

And you know what? Their faith held up. They counted on God's merciful intervention, and time and time again He provided what was most needed at exactly the right moment.

Believe me, I can see how a person who wasn't looking at my situation through eyes of faith could have viewed it. I got "lucky" that my gas tank wasn't full. It was a "coincidence" that my truck skimmed past an immovable object and was slowed by lesser objects. Because Methodist Hospital was where NASCAR drivers who competed on the Indianapolis Motor Speedway were taken after crashes, I "benefited" from the skills of some of the best medical professionals in the country. And if I didn't know God through Christ, I'd likely view my circumstances the same way.

But I do happen to know a God who is gracious. And on that day, my family and I thanked Him for Dr. Jones. For knitting him together in his mother's womb. For gifting him with intellect, skill, hard work, and determination, and for making his highly skilled hands available to me within hours of my father's desperate plea.

CHAPTER 8

HEALING

Surgeons operating on my eye socket and grafting healthy skin back onto my body weren't the only helpers God was using. I was also beginning multiple therapies every day to help rehabilitate me. Daily, after I'd eaten breakfast and my bandages were changed, I'd either receive a visit from a speech therapist or occupational therapist in my room, or I'd be transferred to a wheelchair and wheeled down to a treatment venue.

Three weeks after I arrived, I had my first whirlpool treatment, in which nurses scrubbed the dead skin and scabs off my wounds. That process of scrubbing would increase circulation and speed up the drainage from the wounds. After wheeling me to the tub, my nurse, Kurt, removed my bandages and with the help of another aid lowered me into the whirlpool so the warm water could cleanse my healing skin. Unfortunately, that first treatment took place on one of those days when I was drugged up and I became a little agitated. By the time they hoisted me out of the water and set me down to replace my dressings with my mom's assistance, I was not having any of it. Suffice to say that I shouted out some ugly words my mother had certainly never heard me utter, telling them what they could do with themselves.

While my terse profanity was crystal clear, my speech during those first weeks was pretty difficult to discern. Syllables were stilted. I wasn't always able to put words together well. Sometimes I'd have a thought in my head that I just couldn't articulate well. So the words that passed my lips didn't always match what I wanted to say. Sometimes my speech would be so slurred that even my parents had a hard time understanding me. Eventually, though, Mom picked up my weird new vernacular, and if visitors struggled to understand me, she was always nearby to interpret.

What no one could predict was how much or how little improvement I'd make over time. There was simply no way to parse out what might be related to a concussion that would eventually heal, what was a result of being heavily medicated, and what might be the ongoing effects of a traumatic brain injury. Hopeful and trusting God for my healing, my parents erred on the side of optimism. Of course I'd bounce back and return to being the Mike they once knew who didn't curse at helpful medical professionals.

Right?

During a whirlpool treatment a week later, I saw panic wash over the faces of the two nurses who were scrubbing my legs. One was Kurt and the other was a young female nurse whom I found particularly attractive. Following their gaze toward the water in the whirlpool, I noticed it was brown. I'd had diarrhea and hadn't even realized it because of the medication I was taking.

They quickly lifted me out of the water. The scene that would have mortified any teenage boy was particularly dangerous for me because of the bacteria in the feces making contact with all the open sores on my legs; that could quickly lead to infection.

The nurses lowered me into a plastic chair, and one invited my dad over to be with me while they treated my legs. As Kurt went to prepare what was needed for the procedure, the other nurse prepped me for what was to come.

"Mike," she explained, "because of what just happened, there's a high risk of infection, and we can't afford for your legs to get infected."

Though she didn't say it, I already understood that a serious infection could lead to amputation.

"So we need to clean your legs, and the way we do that is by pouring a saline solution over them." She didn't pull any punches, warning me, "This is going to hurt."

That didn't seem good.

Kurt returned with two buckets of warm saline solution and said, "I want you to close your eyes and hold your dad's hand."

Then, swiftly and thoroughly, they drenched my legs with the saline solution. And even though I'd been warned what was coming, nothing could have prepared me for the excruciating pain of salt literally being poured in my wounds. I screamed.

When they finished, I looked up to see tears seeping from my dad's eyes.

"Mike," he said, "it's over. I know that was rough and I'm so proud of you."

The procedure was excruciating. For both of us.

Because I was an athlete, I *did* know what it meant to work hard, and I was committed to doing my part to recover as quickly as I could.

The day after the brutal whirlpool treatment, I still felt wiped out. After breakfast, I fell asleep. I was awakened by my mom letting me know I had work to do.

"Mike," she said gently, "it's time for occupational therapy."

It was my first session. I didn't know exactly what that meant, so she explained that occupational therapists help people with various challenges to execute their daily routines. Mine—Sharon—would determine whether or not I'd be able to feed myself, brush my teeth, and dress myself.

"Today," Sharon explained, "I'll just be doing an assessment to get a baseline on how you're functioning."

Still a little groggy, I nodded in agreement.

She started by asking me some really basic questions about myself and my injury, then moved on to harder stuff.

"Now let's talk about shapes," Sharon suggested. Showing me a flashcard with the word "square" on it, she asked, "How many sides does this square have?"

If I'd been in my right mind, I would have made some wisecrack about feeling like a preschooler.

"Four. I'm pretty sure. Four."

I thought I saw my mom laugh.

The therapist made a note in her binder.

Then, showing me a card with the word "triangle" on it, Sharon asked, "And how many sides does a triangle have?" she asked.

"Triangle…" I mused. "Triangle …?"

"Yes, how many sides does this triangle have?"

"It definitely has sides," I confirmed. "But I'm not sure how many."

A look of concern flashed across Mom's face. Let's not even get into what happened with the hexagons and octagons.

After testing my brain, Sharon tested my body.

Inviting me to hold my hand on the tabletop in front of me as if I were playing a piano, she asked me to lift my index finger.

With a wellspring of confidence, I lifted the index finger of my right hand.

"And how about your middle finger?" she prompted.

Looking at my right hand, I could see my middle finger, but it wouldn't move.

"Wait, is this some kind of trick?" I asked, thinking it might be some hypnosis party game.

"No trick," she said. "Just lift your middle finger."

I'd never had to think about willing a finger to move, or an arm, or a leg. And suddenly, no amount of mental energy directed toward my finger could convince it to budge.

"Oh my gosh," I gasped. "I really can't lift it?"

I heard my own voice crackle with fear. The number of limitations I was facing seemed to be growing each day instead of shrinking.

"Don't worry about it," Sharon said, "your brain and body are still healing. We'll keep working on it."

"It'll be okay, Mike," Mom reassured me. "You'll get there."

I continued the assessment of tasks a preschooler could have nailed with his eyes closed. I could open a book, turn a page, and even put on an Indiana Pacers hat.

But I didn't care if I could put on a hat. What I cared about was being able to lead worship while playing the guitar.

A nurse's aide brought a tray of food for lunch just as Sharon finished her assessment.

"You did great, Mike," she said. "I'll be back tomorrow and we'll try again."

As the aid arranged a warm plate of meatloaf, green beans, and white rice in front of me, I looked to my mom.

"Mom," I said dejectedly. "I'm a mess. How am I going to lead worship if I *literally* can't lift a finger?"

Shifting seamlessly from worried-mom mode into nurse mode, she explained, "It's still early in your recovery, Mike. You have a long way to go, but you'll get there."

I accepted the encouragement, but I knew that we really didn't know how much function I'd regain in the wake of the accident. Nothing had happened physically to limit my finger, which meant my brain was the problem.

And although neither my nurse nor anyone in my family was willing to see it or discuss it, there was a chance that long after my eye socket had healed and my burns had scarred over, my brain would continue to give me trouble.

The thought of not recovering from my brain injury was pretty scary. I'd seen other patients with brain injuries in the halls of the pediatric intensive care unit. Some had suffered them at birth. Another patient in one of my therapy sessions who'd been in a wheelchair most of his life would have loud outbursts of yelling and cursing. Though I tried to roll with it, the truth was that the unpredictable explosions scared me. There was also a girl my age who'd been in a car accident like me. She'd rolled her car five times and suffered massive injuries to her body and brain, and hers was permanent. She couldn't even lift her head or respond to her mom.

Both of them reminded me of the kids at school relegated to special education classrooms. A few attended my church. I didn't know them well, but I did understand intuitively the stigma teens endured who weren't neurotypical. I'd seen these kids teased on the bus and after gym class. And while I never would have made fun of a student with autism or Down syndrome, I didn't feel entirely comfortable around them, either. I wasn't exactly sure what to say or do. While I never really thought about it until my hospitalization, I did believe that, as someone who thought and learned and spoke like a typical adolescent, I was fundamentally different than they were.

Or was I?

I didn't know anymore.

When I was trapped in my truck, Matt didn't know if I was dead or alive. And if I was alive, he certainly didn't know the degree to which I would or wouldn't recover. And while I was in the hospital, no one could predict how much my body and brain would or would not improve. There were certainly landmark moments we celebrated, like a successful skin graft or the first time I stood to use the restroom, but none of us could say for sure how far I would progress.

TRUSTING GOD MOMENT BY MOMENT

For many who suffer life's trials, there is no way to know what the future holds. No way to know if aggressive chemo will knock out the dangerous cancer cells. No way to know if the grief over the loss of a child will ever make way to welcome another. No way to know if a sudden financial crisis will limit dreams for the future. When we're in the fire, when we're choking on smoky fumes, we can't see clearly. We can't hear clearly. We can't think clearly.

What we can do is choose to trust God moment by moment. That's what I saw my parents do throughout my recovery. I saw them choose to trust God one day at a time. When a finger refuses to budge, we trust that God is with us. When a bodily malfunction threatens our safety, we trust that God is still good. When our thoughts are jumbled, we trust that we're in God's care. Although we love the kind of fairytale stories where all conflicts are resolved and a happy couple lives happily ever after, the real struggles we face aren't typically smoothed out in ninety minutes.

So we trust God, finger by finger, threat by threat, and thought by thought. In each moment we choose to trust that God is with us.

CHAPTER 9

THE WHO?

One Wednesday night in October, a passerby drifting down the hallway past my room and peeking inside would have been in for a real treat. That night, all the guys in my life group came to visit me on the evening we'd typically meet.

"Hey brah," John greeted me first, "you are lookin' good!"

We laughed because I was definitely not looking good. Though I wasn't as messed up as Matt remembered, I had no shirt on, three of my limbs were bandaged, and I had the ol' noodle up my nose.

The guys encircling my bed were dressed head to toe in mustard-yellow scrubs to keep me safe from infection. Sam, who served in Northview's worship band with me, brought his guitar and Matt, John, and Jason, whose dad was our church's mission pastor, had come, too. These were my boys.

As Sam strummed and we sang "Here I Am to Worship," I closed my eyes and allowed myself to transport mentally to North-view's Barn on Sunday evening. In my imagination, I had no head injury, no burns, and no broken bones. I was a typical healthy kid playing my guitar and leading my friends in worshiping Jesus. Every time I stepped on that stage, I spoke, prayed, and sang of my trust in Jesus. And as I opened my eyes again and glanced at the bandages on my body and monitors at my side, I became keenly aware that *this*—this hospital room, in the wake of my accident—was where the rubber hit the road. Given the opportunity to trust Jesus with my body, my brain, and my future, would I? Could I? With no assurance that I would leave the hospital with both my legs, I couldn't even imagine what my future would look like. And yet I was keenly aware that I had been given an opportunity to live out my trust in Jesus. And I wanted nothing more than to honor Him with my life.

After a few songs I asked, "Hey Sam, can I play?"

"Of course, man," Sam quickly answered, handing me the guitar.

Sitting up in bed, resting the guitar on my lap, my left hand explored the strings on its neck. My left hand had been burned more severely than my right, making the process of finding familiar positions painful. But I pushed through because I was so eager to play again. I used Sam's pick to gingerly strum the chords of the song we'd been singing.

The guys and my mom joined me in singing, and when the song ended everyone broke out in applause. And rightly so! A few days earlier I couldn't even lift my middle finger on command, but somehow the muscle memory in my body bypassed my brain—and not only was I able to play the instrument, but I remembered every word of the song. The process of playing and singing had been stored away in my deep places and was easier to retrieve than any of us had expected.

But notes and lyrics weren't the only familiar experience. The nearness I felt to God while worshiping was also a gift. For weeks I'd struggled against both drugs and a brain injury to focus on anything, but in that space of worship I finally experienced the deep connection to God that I'd known before the accident. So while my soul was definitely fed by the presence of my friends, it was also being fed by the One who had been present with me in every groggy, painful moment.

When the applause for my stellar performance died down, Matt's eyes flew open as he seemed to remember something.

"Mike!" he shouted. "You're never going to believe what happened the other night!"

Having no clue whether he'd gone on a date or won the lottery, I was eager to hear.

"Mrs. Kinney," he said, turning to my mom, "you gotta hear this!"

So maybe it wasn't a date.

"So I've had my clothes from the accident hanging on my wall in my bedroom. They haven't been washed since the accident. I just hung them up so I could see them and remember the awesome thing God had done."

We all nodded in affirmation.

"And the other night I pulled them off the wall, I put them to my face, and I could smell the soot and ash."

We listened intently.

"And as I was holding them, I felt something in the pocket."

He paused, no doubt for dramatic effect, but the suspense was too much.

"What was it?!" Sam exploded.

Matt said, "I could tell that it was something crumpled up, and when I pulled it out, it was two wadded up five-dollar bills."

The guys' faces, and my mom's, were blank.

"So what?" John asked.

"So…" Matt explained, "when Mike and I stopped for gas, he didn't have any money. I didn't have any money in my wallet, but I stuck my hands in both pockets of my shorts looking for money, and only found five dollars."

"And…?" Sam asked, not understanding the significance.

"And," Matt said patiently, "I actually had *fifteen dollars* in my pocket. And if I'd found it, I would have given it to Mike for gas. And that meant there would have been seven or eight more gallons of fuel in his truck that would have exploded when it caught on fire."

I could see my friends' eyes grow wide.

"It's almost like it saved his life," Matt finished.

Because she knew Matt had had no intention of leaving me, no matter what happened, my mom turned to him and added, "And *your* life."

"Wow," Jason marveled, "that's pretty awesome."

"Totally," I agreed.

"God is so rad," John said.

After chatting a bit longer, the guys said goodbye and left. It felt weird that while they could just walk out the door, hop in a car, and go back home to play video games, my life felt frozen in time. They'd started school, kept going to youth group, were busy with activities, and were thinking ahead to life after high school.

Me? In the wake of their visit, I was thinking about how great it would feel just to walk. And one day walk out of the hospital.

The next week, I was resting in bed after completing my therapies for the day when Matt and his mom, Joni, dipped into my room. They both sported wide grins on their faces, and for some reason, Joni was carrying a big fishbowl. I couldn't imagine what it was for, but one thing I learned quickly was that our family was being loved in generous ways.

At Northview Church, Jesus's command to love one another the way He loved us was lived out beautifully. I'd certainly tasted it before my accident, as I watched the congregation rally around other families in need, but I don't think we could have predicted the response to my accident. When those earliest friends and family who'd gathered to pray in the emergency room went home, they continued to love on my family. Reba and a few friends from youth group cleaned our home. Others helped to arrange John's care and transportation to and from school and football practice. Meals magically showed up in our freezer. More meals were brought to the hospital for my family. The feasts were so abundant that my mom would often create a spread in the PICU waiting room to feed other visitors.

And guess who kept our yard neatly mowed while I was in the hospital? Josh McClain, the bully who'd made a crack in the school parking lot about my mowing gear. Although for a few months my parents assumed a well-meaning neighbor had been tending to the yard, one of the other swim team moms eventually revealed that it had been Josh all along.

Beaming as she approached my bed, Joni proudly handed me the large fishbowl with a sign that said, "Picks for Kinney."

"What is this?" I asked, seeing colorful guitar picks inside the bowl.

Joni, who owned a local Christian bookstore, explained, "We invited anyone to offer a guitar pick with a Scripture verse or encouragement, and they have just poured in! *The Bob & Tom Radio Show* announced it on-air, and they just keep coming!"

Reba Cooper was an administrator at the local private school attended by the children of radio personality Tom Griswold. He was half of the popular syndicated *Bob & Tom* radio duo. So when Tom went to the office one day, Reba told him about Picks for Kinney and asked if he could mention it on the air. Tom was all for it and generated lots of buzz and excitement about the effort.

My mom came closer to look at the picks as I began to pull them out one by one, reading what each stranger had written. Some bore slogans of encouragement. Others had Scripture verses. And on some, strangers had used very thin Sharpie markers to write the tiniest little notes of love you've ever seen. I was blown away by the incredible support I was receiving from people I didn't even know.

"Dude, it's been so cool to see people get psyched about this," Matt said. "There are so many people praying for you, you wouldn't believe it."

He was right. It was hard to believe. And yet in every plastic pick, spaghetti casserole, and carefully chosen Hallmark card that flooded my room, God was showing me His love through His people.

God was also about to show me His love through another, very unlikely, someone.

The Saturday after Matt and Joni brought me Picks for Kinney, my parents came to spend the day with me. Dad was carrying a big box.

"Hey, guys," I said. I was feeling pretty good that day.

"Hi, honey," Mom cooed.

"Hey, Mike," Dad said with a big grin on his face. "I have a surprise for you."

He pulled out something bulky wrapped in a blanket. Pulling it back, I saw it was covering a new guitar.

"Dad...thank—"

"Nope," he interrupted, "it's not from me."

Still clutching the guitar, he pulled out a piece of paper and handed it to me.

The letterhead on the stationery signaled that it was from someone named Pete Townshend—whoever that was. The note read:

> *Heard about your accident via* Bob & Tom *and I'm sending you this guitar, which I very much hope you will be able to play soon. I pray for you and your family and hope for a speedy recovery.*

What on earth?!

"A guitar?!" I asked dumbfounded. "Who is this guy?!"

"Mike, it's Pete Townshend. The Who."

"The who?" I asked. "That's what I want to know."

"No," Dad clarified, "he's from the rock band The Who. They were a pretty big deal in classic rock."

It was clear from my dad's face that he admired this guy and was blown away by the gift.

Apparently, someone on the *Bob & Tom* team had reached out to Pete Townshend—the founder and lead guitarist of the legendary '60s and '70s rock band. When he learned that my guitar had been burned up in the accident, he had sent me a guitar. Me! Seventeen-year-old Michael W. Kinney of Noblesville, Indiana.

The large, heavy, well-insured, and carefully packaged box had arrived at our home just a few weeks after the accident, when I was still too disoriented to be able to receive it for the wonder it was. Dad had opened the box postmarked from London and discovered the treasure inside.

Once he was convinced that I understood the magnitude of the gift and the notoriety of the giver, he held up the guitar so I could read the inscription scribbled across its body: "To Mike, this is the Phoenix. Pete Townshend."

According to Greek mythology, a bird called the Phoenix dies in flames of self-combustion, and then is reborn from the ashes. Like the myth, the guitar I'd just been given had been birthed from the ashes of my accident. And, to my ear, it echoed my own death and resurrection, as well as that of Another. While both Townshend and the symbol of the phoenix were, at the time, new to me, the deep, reverberating meaning of the gift was immediately evident.

When my dad handed me the guitar, I sat up a bit straighter in bed so I could play it. The fire had burned my hand, thumb, knuckles, and arm, so I gingerly guarded my hurt places as I began to play the chords of "Open the Eyes of My Heart," pressing them with my left hand and strumming gently with my right.

When I glanced at my mom's face, her eyes were wide.

"What?" I asked her. "What are you looking at?"

"Wayne," she said, ignoring me and turning to my father, "remember how I told you that in physical therapy he couldn't lift his finger on cue, but that he played with Matt and the boys?"

"I do," he confirmed.

"Isn't it amazing?" she asked. "The doctor told me this afternoon that the area of his brain that was injured should have affected his ability to play music."

My dad watched as I continued to strum my new axe.

"Praise God!" he exclaimed.

Even in my tender state, it felt amazing to be playing and singing. It felt like I was doing what I was made to do.

Word began to spread throughout the hospital about the gift I'd received. Sometimes staff members would pop their heads in the door to get a peek at the Phoenix. One nurse from a different floor was so taken by it that I suggested he play it.

"I could never!" he retorted. "You need to put it in a glass case and not let anyone touch it."

I heard what he was saying, but I was definitely going to play that guitar.

If you stripped away the celebrity status of the giver, that guitar meant just one thing to me: I had a second chance. And I was going to make it through the fire and rise from the ashes.

CHAPTER 10

NORMAL, NOT NORMAL

Even if I had been in my right mind during those first weeks in the hospital, I wouldn't have been able to recount the endless parade of visitors who showed me love and support.

The Sorum family—our family's "BFFs"—had moved to South Dakota two years earlier. Despite the miles, our families had stayed in touch. After my accident, I'd learned from my parents that Jamie, the oldest, wasn't the carefree, silly girl she'd been when we were kids. She struggled with depression. She was often restless. A year before my accident, she'd downed a bottle of Tylenol in an attempt to end her life. The Sorums didn't understand Jamie's behavior, but they got her a counselor to try to help her figure out why she was acting out. Despite those struggles, Jim, Pat, Jamie, Micah, and Jacob had driven all the way from South Dakota to visit me in the hospital.

That was an amazing reminder of the happy times we'd shared. Pat was like a second mom to me. Jamie was joyful, and Jacob was the silly kid I remembered him to be. We found ourselves laughing over almost nothing. While I shared with Jamie some of the details about my accident, John and Jacob played a card game on the floor, and our moms talked in hushed tones. When they saw my sleepy eyes start to droop, they gently withdrew, heading back to our house to prepare dinner for my family. I treasured the time with them because, unlike the nurses, doctors, aides, and therapists who'd become my new family, I felt seen, known, and loved by each of the Sorums.

A decade earlier, when the six of us kids had been running around the church like wild monkeys, none of us could have imagined the kinds of challenges we'd one day face. There had been no traces of Jamie's mental health issues. And of course, we couldn't have predicted, nor would we ever have dreamed, that I'd have what seemed like a freak accident for which there was no clear cause other than me being tired. But we weathered them together across the miles.

Not long after the Sorums left, my mom helped me into a wheelchair and wheeled me over to the expansive window at the edge of my room to look outside as the sun began to set. It's the first time I remember seeing the outdoors after the accident. White puffy clouds dotted the crisp blue sky. The occasional bird darted past. And the sounds of traffic reminded me that, while my life had come to an abrupt halt when I'd slammed into a telephone pole, the lives of others continued on. When they returned to South Dakota, the Sorum kids would keep going to school, attending soccer practice, playing the piano, and spending time with friends. I didn't begrudge them their normalcy, but I sure missed mine. And I wondered if I'd ever be normal again.

That said, I was aware that I wasn't the only Kinney whose "normal" had been affected by my accident. While Rachel was at her second year at Taylor University, my brother John, was caught in the whirlwind our lives became in the wake of August 16 as he began eighth grade.

Sitting beside me in front of the expansive window, Mom caught a glimpse of him out of the corner of her eye.

"John," she ordered sternly, "put those back."

Dutifully, John reluctantly returned the box of latex gloves he'd found in a cabinet in my hospital room.

One day John had been the child of an involved dad and a mom who was often at home caring for him, and the next day he was being shuttled all over town by generous folks in our community as my parents kept vigil by my bedside. It was no secret that my accident had a huge impact on him.

John had been in summer training as a member of the Noblesville Middle School football team when he broke his arm. A few days later, my accident brought the world's sympathy for his broken arm to an abrupt halt, eclipsed by my more severe injuries. When he came to visit me in those early days, his right arm was in a cast, as was my left and both legs. Together, we were quite a sight.

Because my mom was so committed to staying with me and monitoring my care, John would often be stuck visiting me, too. When Mom and I were distracted by other visitors, John usually was messing around with any equipment he could get his hands on. If there was a button that could be pushed, he'd push it. He'd ask Mom questions about the way different medical gadgets worked.

And whatever my mom needed for my care—towels, ice chips, gauze—John would find and fetch it for her. He made the most of a situation no sibling would ever willingly sign on for.

It was a gift that family and friends all pitched in to help keep his life going. When he'd visit, I'd hear him griping to my dad about football, or telling my mom about an algebra test, or about his friend who liked a girl. It felt like John's life, and *everybody's* life, continued while mine had been put on pause. I spent so much time sleeping as a result of the drugs I was being given, I truly have few personal memories of those early weeks. I'd lost that season of my life when I should have been starting my senior year of high school. That momentum had come to a halt on August 16.

I was stuck. And I was reminded again of my stuckness by someone who reminded me of my most active self.

I was listening to music on a Friday evening when Coach Busby from my swim team popped his head into my doorway.

"Coach!" I shouted when I saw him.

"Kinney!" he hollered back at me.

Hopping up, Mom offered Coach her chair. Before he could decline, she offered, "I've been meaning to stretch my legs, and this is my chance. Sit down." She stepped into the hallway to give us some privacy.

Settling in beside me, Coach told me that all the guys missed me.

"I miss them, too," I said. "Boy, I want to be able swim this season."

I'd been elected team co-captain over the summer and had been hoping to beat my best times and make it to the state finals again.

"We all want you out there with us," he said.

The sobering reality was that the length of my recovery—and even whether I would fully recover—was still unknown.

Sullenly, I admitted, "Coach, I don't even know if I'll walk again, and I have no idea about swimming. I guess that means I can't be a team captain."

I searched his face for signs of the disappointment I felt, but I didn't see it.

"You're right," he said, to my disappointment. Then he added, "As long as you're in this bed, you can't be a captain."

Now he was just rubbing it in.

"But once you get back on the pool deck, you're team captain whether you're on crutches, or in a wheelchair, or whatever."

His words gave me the hope I needed on that day and in that season. And they'd continue to echo in my heart and mind during my daily therapies. In addition to gunning to lead worship again at Northview, Coach Busby had given me another great reason to work as hard as I could.

Coach had been in touch with my parents and already knew that the injury to my Achilles tendon meant that it had shortened and would be chronically tight.

"That's why I want you to keep working in PT," he said, "and I want to see you work on getting back some flexibility in your Achilles."

"I'll do it," I promised. "I'll keep working hard."

Coach filled me in on how some of the other swimmers had been doing and, before he left, encouraged me to keep pushing.

Though our visit had been brief, Coach had given me a gift. Because I now had a second little snapshot stored in my heart that

I could peek at for inspiration: a thumbnail of me on the pool deck. It wasn't yet clear whether I was there in a chair, cheering on my teammates, or as a competitor. But it inspired me. It was a needed little glimpse of "normal."

When we face challenges in our lives, whatever we knew as "normal" often shifts. Sometimes we know that the disaster we're facing will be temporary: the smoke damage to our home will be repaired and we'll move back in; it'll take longer than expected to save money for that final semester of school, but we'll still graduate; rest and good nutrition will heal our bodies and we'll return to work.

But other times, the "normal" we took for granted and expected to always enjoy will look very different from that point forward. In fact, nothing about our new lives feels normal at all. We ask the restaurant hostess for a table for one instead of a table for two. We honor the birth of child who's no longer alive. We wear a prosthetic where a fleshy limb once was. Against our will, we move into a new "normal" that we never would have chosen.

In the hospital, I was still figuring out what my new "normal" would look like. I knew that for the rest of my life, my body would bear scars. Though I still hoped to walk, I knew my abilities would be limited by the damage the flames had done to my lower legs. I didn't know the extent to which my brain would recover. Like any adolescent, I wanted more than anything to fit in. To be accepted. To be normal.

I couldn't yet envision what that would look like.

Each day, when a nurse would tenderly change the dressings on my legs, I would look away. I'd grown accustomed to busying myself with conversation, a book, television, or anything else during the painful daily ritual. The truth was, I didn't want to look at my legs. I knew they would never look like they once had, and I didn't want to face it.

But one afternoon when I was feeling daring, I *looked*. Tight scar tissue had formed at the seams where skin from my back and thighs had been grafted to the surface of my leg where the old skin had been burned off. Some of it was discolored, like jigsaw pieces jammed together that didn't quite fit right. The scarred flesh covered most of my right leg and about half of my left. My mind couldn't keep my worries at bay. *What will people think? What will girls think? Will they be grossed out? Will my legs ever look better than they do now?* My face must have registered my concern, because the nurse wearing purple scrubs who was treating me asked how I was doing.

"It's same as usual," I said. "I'm OK. Just thinking about the scars."

"I get that," she said. "Actually, although you can't see them when I'm wearing my scrubs, I have scars from an accident when I was younger."

I wondered what had caused the scars, but I didn't ask.

"Really?" I asked, curious.

"Yeah," she said, "and for a lot of years I hated them."

That tracks, I thought.

"But," she continued, "today I see them differently. Today I see them as battle wounds that I'm proud of. They remind me where I was, and remind me that I'm strong, and I'm brave, and I made it."

Strength resonated in her voice.

"That's pretty cool," I said, considering what she'd shared. I already knew what someone who was just trying to make me feel better sounded like, and this was not that. I believed her because she'd been where I was.

In that moment I decided that I would not be ashamed of my battle scars. I'd embrace them as my new normal.

CHAPTER 11

Moving Forward

Am I awake or dreaming?

Covered by only a few thin sheets, I am freezing cold. I realize I'm in an elevator on a hospital gurney, accompanied by a man in scrubs I've never seen before. I know I've been in the hospital, but I don't know where I'm being taken. Because I'm not hooked up to any pain meds or sleepy juice, as I would be if I were heading into surgery, I assume it must be someplace benign.

This is the first clear memory following my accident that is fully my own.

As we exited the elevator on the sixth floor, the orderly wheeled me past a nurses' station and down an unfamiliar hallway painted in bright primary colors. When he pivoted and tipped me past a door that read "6363," I realized that it must be my new room because I'd "graduated" from the PICU. I saw the banners, posters, signs, and cards that had been hanging in my first room, the cacophony of color and shapes and well-wishes communicating that I was not alone. There was an entire community supporting me and my recovery.

Above the bed was a sign made from blue foam board, with rounded pre-cut foam lettering reading, "Michael W." The sign made me feel known and loved.

Though I wasn't home yet, I was one step closer. While I'd been in the PICU, I'd chosen not to look carefully at the damage that the fire had done my body. But in the wake of my encounter with the kind nurse who also lived with burns, I decided that if I was going to own and embrace my battle wounds, I was going to have to get to know them.

Not long after leaving the PICU, on the morning before a surgery to plug up a hole I'd worked into my heel, I watched closely as my nurse carefully wrapped my legs after a whirlpool therapy. Grafts of scarred skin had been patchworked together. My muscles had atrophied, and my lower leg was now thin. It wasn't pretty. But I was prepared.

"They're bad," I told my mom, "but they'll get better."

I said it as much to convince myself as to comfort her.

"Hey, Mom," I asked, "do you think I'm going to be able to swim this year?"

She hesitated before answering, "I think we just don't know yet. It may not be possible."

I wasn't walking, and had just gained the ability to push myself a bit in a wheelchair.

"I know my Achilles is bad," I mused, "but I guess I always thought that swimming would be possible."

"And it might be, but right now it's not."

"And you know homecoming is in three weeks," I continued. "I can't believe I'm missing homecoming my senior year."

The weight of the losses was heavier than I could carry. Falling back onto my pillow, I began to cry.

"Honey," Mom said, "I'm so sorry."

Though I could tell she was trying to hide it, I heard the tears in her voice, too.

"I'm so sorry you're missing things you love, but so, so grateful that you're still here with us."

The consolation meant little to me.

That afternoon in surgery, the doctor did some final skin grafts on my right leg, loosened my tight Achilles, positioned my foot at ninety degrees, and then plugged the spot on my left heel. When I woke up in my own room, my youth pastor, Don, had come to visit. I still felt a little woozy.

"Hey, man," I said with a smile.

"Mike Kinney," he replied with a grin, "it is so good to see you."

Don had showed up at the emergency room the night of my accident and had been a faithful visitor throughout my hospitalization.

"Good to see you, too," I answered. "What's new?"

He thought for a minute and then said, "Well, we're gearing up for the fall retreat."

It was all he had to say. Every year two hundred kids from Northview went on a weekend retreat to Kentucky. The previous year I'd helped to lead worship, and I dreamed of being up there again, strumming my new guitar.

Mom had given Don and me some privacy, but I called out to her in the hallway. "Mom, say I can go to the fall retreat! Didn't the doctors say that I could, like, go home for a weekend? This would basically be the same thing."

Even I knew that wasn't true. Whatever energy and skills it took to navigate a mountain retreat in another state were wildly different from those required to wheel me up the ramp that had been built to our front door and dump me onto our living room couch.

"Mike," she said sympathetically, "your dad and I don't think it's going to work this year, but we'll consider it."

Perceiving how the conversation could head south pretty quickly, Don redirected my attention by telling me about the new students who'd joined the worship team. I understood the situation was awkward, so I let the idea of the retreat go. For the moment. After Don left, I continued to think about it...and whether or not I could sneak out of the hospital, hijack an ambulance from outside the ER, and find my way to Kentucky.

A guy could dream.

For the seven weeks I was in the hospital, I was transported to therapies in a wheelchair and surgeries on a gurney. In the earliest weeks, I used a catheter and bedpan, but eventually my mom could help me into a wheelchair and wheel me to the bathroom. What I hadn't done yet, however, was walk.

In therapy, I'd been working on building up some of the strength and muscle mass I'd lost from being bedbound for almost two months. The first week of October, my physical therapist, Beth, gave me the opportunity to try taking a few steps with a walker. Mom sat at the edge of the room, looking on.

"OK," Beth said, "I'm going to help you to stand, and then I want you to grip the walker and just find your balance."

With Beth supporting me, I pushed myself up from the wheelchair to a standing position. Shifting my grip to the walker, I stood upright, feeling a little weak. I knew I'd dropped from 160 pounds down to 117. Keenly aware of the strength I'd lost in my arms and legs, I felt the way old people look—frail.

"Great job, Mike," Beth said. "Just practice standing."

I knew what practice was. Practice was sprinting 100 meters in the pool. It wasn't *standing*.

"So…" I queried, "I just stand here?"

"For a minute," she said, "yes. Your body needs time to readjust. To remember what it's supposed to do."

In one of the mirrors that spanned the length of the room, I caught a glimpse of my mom's face. She looked as proud as if I'd won the 100-meter freestyle.

"Okay," Beth said, "now I want you to try to take a step or two."

I wanted to impress her by taking a lap around the room, but I realized I was more compromised than I knew. I took two steps and then paused.

"Mike, that's great!" she said. "How do you feel?"

"Weird," I admitted. "Kind of like Jell-O."

"That sounds about right," Beth agreed.

After working a bit longer, I was happy to fall back into the wheelchair and have my mom push me back to my room.

"Honey," she raved, "I'm so proud of you!"

"So it sounds like I can go on the fall retreat, then?"

She sighed. "Mike, you know that might not be possible. Just keep working, and we'll let the doctors decide."

"I think that's a 'yes'!" I said.

I suddenly had a new reason to give my all to therapy. Yes, I'd been working hard at all of it so I could start and finish my senior year of high school. Yes, I was eager to go back onto the pool deck. But the possibility of going on the fall retreat? Now I was giving 300 percent.

When we're stuck, we're often eager to see progress. We're waiting to receive the phone call from the new employer offering us the job. We want the doctor to offer a clean bill of health. We yearn for the broken relationship to be magically mended. We beg for the addiction to evaporate. And yet our plans aren't always the same as God's.

In the fifty-fifth chapter of the book of Isaiah, the author shares the Lord's words, saying, "For as the heavens are higher than the earth, so are my ways higher than your ways, and my thoughts than your thoughts" (Isaiah 55:9). So true! Had any divine entity consulted me, I would have scripted the whole accident and recovery very differently. And honestly, some days it was hard to see what God was up to. Recovery was much slower and more tedious than I would have preferred. I *didn't* understand why God didn't hasten things along.

I was weary of hospital living and eager to get home.

CHAPTER 12

HOMECOMING-ISH

The first week of October, the doctors let me out of hospital jail for eight hours.

My family had converted a first-floor office into a bedroom for me so I wouldn't have to face the stairs to my second-floor bedroom, which I couldn't yet manage. "Home" never felt so good. My family watched the Colts game. I spent some time in my room playing guitar. Jason came over. And my folks even wheeled me into youth group at the Barn! It felt surreal to see all my friends there. Many were eager to see me and welcome me back. Others shied away, as if they didn't quite know what to say or do. I guess I get that. Naturally, seeing the old crew leading worship, with a few new members, ignited my passion to lead again. Before my folks and I left, I approached Don.

"Mike," he said, beaming, "it's so awesome to see you here!"

"Thanks, man," I answered. "I've been working hard to get out of that joint and be here again."

"Well keep doing what you're doing," Don said encouragingly.

"So…" I suggested, "if I can get a pass next weekend, could I lead worship with you guys?"

"Are you kidding?" he asked. "That would be awesome. I hope to see you at rehearsal."

That week, intent on dazzling the doctors who would have to sign off on another get-out-of-jail-free card, I gave 500 percent to all my therapies. And it worked! I was allowed to go home for two whole days.

Rachel was home for the weekend, and after a delicious steak dinner as a family, my parents loaded me into the minivan to go to the Noblesville High football game.

I was more nervous than I thought I would be. *What will my peers think? Will the wheelchair freak them out? Will they talk to me? Will they pity me?* I felt like a middle schooler on the first day at a new school. And I didn't hate that the cool October weather gave me an excuse to wear clothes over all my burns. I knew I wouldn't be able to sit with my friends because of the wheelchair, but I was still excited to be around peers who hadn't suffered life-altering traumas. The evening, I decided, would be normal…ish.

My dad dropped me and Mom off near the entrance to the field, then parked the van in a handicapped parking space. When he rejoined us, we entered through the ticket booth. Since we couldn't even make it up the few steps to the first row of bleachers, we were directed toward a swinging metal gate next to the track.

We'd missed kickoff, but a few minutes into the first half, while the two teams were huddled up strategizing, my parents wheeled me toward the sea of black and gold that was the Noblesville cheering section. Scanning the crowd, I saw a bunch of my swim buddies in their usual spot in the student section near the top of the bleachers. It's where I should have been. When one of them spotted me, he began to chant.

"Kin-ney's back, Kin-ney's back…"

The rest of the team joined him, and then other students began to chime in.

"Kin-ney's BACK! Kin-ney's BACK!"

Feeling a little sheepish, I lifted my arm to acknowledge the love.

Soon hundreds of students were chanting along, "KIN-NEY'S BACK! KIN-NEY'S BACK!"

I felt Mom give my shoulder a squeeze.

When the shrill pitch of the ref's whistle announced that play was resuming, the students' revelry softened and their attention returned to the field.

But the rhythmic cadence of their welcome continued to pulse in my heart. As a volunteer handed my parents two folding chairs to sit beside me, I continued to reflect on the exciting moment. On one hand, I reasoned, being laid up after my accident wasn't so very different than the quarterback who'd had knee surgery the previous year. But another thought continued to nag, hissing that this *was* different. Yes, my body continued to heal, though I knew I'd have a few lasting deficits. Maybe the quarterback would, too. What scared me was what we couldn't yet predict. Especially cognitive issues. My speech was still compromised. Because my mouth wasn't yet cooperating completely, I wasn't able to get words out the way I once had. I spoke slowly. I used fragmented sentences. My family and friends could understand me, but I knew that strangers who spoke to me on the few hospital outings I'd attended with other kids assumed I was intellectually challenged.

Mom had been meeting with the team at the hospital to strategize my eventual discharge. I knew I'd be returning to school in the Exceptional Children's program for students with special needs. I'd join their classroom to get the extra assistance I needed so I could graduate with my class. While I wasn't psyched about it and didn't want other students to see me there, I had no other choice. I was willing to agree to anything that would get me released from the hospital.

As my parents and I watched Noblesville High move the ball down the field, inch by inch and yard by yard, I recognized my own slow progress in reaching my goal of being normal again. I'd been working hard in all my therapies so that my senior year would resemble what I'd always imagined it would be like. I wanted more than anything to meet the guys from my life group at Wendy's and talk about the teachers we hated, the girls we liked, our part-time jobs, and the colleges we hoped to attend. I didn't want to entertain the possibility that, despite all my hard work, I might not reach my goal. Maybe nothing would ever be the same again.

"Hey, Mike," Dad said, interrupting my thoughts, "you want any popcorn? Reese's? A soda?"

"Nah," I shrugged, "I'm good. Thanks."

The fact that my dentist dad was offering me garbage food only confirmed that my world was not yet back to normal. I didn't know if it ever would be.

The next afternoon, I was nervous about returning to youth group to lead worship. It's what I wanted more than anything else, but I knew that I wasn't fully recovered and that others could see that.

At 4:30 p.m., my mom pushed my chair in and my dad carried the guitar I'd received from Pete Townshend. Even though a lot of students couldn't fully appreciate the magnitude of playing on a gift from a legendary performer they'd never heard of, it made me feel like I had a little extra mojo that night.

At the beginning of rehearsal, Don had lowered my mic stand to the height of my face at wheelchair level. When worship began, I let everyone know how great it was to be back and, most of all, to praise God together. Among the songs we sang that night were "The Wonderful Cross," "Your Love, Oh Lord," and "Hope to Carry On." I know it sounds corny, but that night the lyrics had a surprising new depth to my ear.

It felt amazing to be among my people again. For the first time in months, I felt mostly like myself. At the end of the session, as Don was dismissing everyone, he reminded us, "Fall Retreat is in three weeks, and I need your permission forms and checks by next week if you want to go. You don't want to miss it!"

Although I wasn't the best at remembering tasks, I wasn't going to be one of those kids who forgot to turn in this paperwork. And even though I hadn't yet gotten permission from medical staff or my parents, I was all about doing anything it took to go on that retreat.

Returning to the hospital after a weekend at home felt like the bummer it was. I knew that home visits meant I was getting closer to being released, but I was restless to go home for good, return to school, and become normal again.

That week, when I returned to the hospital, the joy of leading worship lingered. I definitely had some other worries, but when I thought about being in the Barn, leading students in prayer and in song, I had a sense that I was being the person God made me to be.

A lot of us who were raised by Christian parents or who grew up in the church were fed Bible stories, Bible songs, prayers, and liturgies. We were shaped by a community of faith. That was certainly my story. Seeing the difference that faith made in the lives of my parents and other leaders I admired at church inspired me to participate in youth group. To lead worship. To join a life group. Before my accident, I was doing everything I could to grow in my faith.

But after my accident, something shifted a bit inside me. It wasn't a change anyone would have even noticed. Suddenly songs about God's saving grace, mercy, and healing were vivified inside me. I wasn't singing about a story I'd heard and believed anymore; I was singing about a story I'd lived. For the first time, my relationship with God was really my own. And while I was pretty consumed in the hospital with tasks like staying awake and learning to walk again, returning home opened up a new space for me to live the reality of what God was doing inside me.

I'd learned in fifth-grade Sunday School that the name "Jesus" means "Yahweh saves." The name combines *Ya*—short for Yahweh, the name of Israel's God—and the verb "*yasha*," meaning "to save, rescue, or deliver." But the person of Jesus was no longer someone who rescued others. He was now the One who rescued me.

When my doctor popped in to visit with me one Tuesday, I was strumming my guitar. I'd left the Phoenix at home, and this one was actually a Takamine, given to me by Tom Griswold of *The Bob & Tom Show*—an exact replica of the one that had burned in my accident.

Entering the room, Dr. Shaw remarked, "Bravo! It's great to hear you playing, Mike."

This pleased me. "Want me to sing you a song?" I asked.

"Absolutely," she said. "Thank you."

My mom offered Dr. Shaw her chair beside my bed and stepped back a bit, as if to honor the sacred, intimate performance.

The song I chose? "Set Me on Fire."

While some might find it a morbid choice—and the fiery lyrics about being covered in kerosene weren't lost on Dr. Shaw—it expressed the burning desire of my heart to live a life that was pleasing to God. Whatever it was that God had for me to do, I wanted to do it. I longed for the Holy Spirit to use my life for His glory. Leading worship on Sunday was certainly one way that I could see God using me. As I thought about finishing high school and moving into college, I didn't know exactly what God's plan for me would look like, but I was open and eager to discover how He would call me to use my gifts to serve Him.

Unwittingly, it seems, I had already begun. The song I shared moved Dr. Shaw. In fact, a few days later she asked my mom if they could meet up for coffee in the cafeteria to talk about our family's faith. When Mom shared this with me, I dared to dream that maybe, just maybe, God would use my music to minister to the people He loved.

The fact that my overnight visit home had been a success meant that doctors were willing to consider releasing me. (I'm sure dazzling Dr. Shaw with my mad performance skills didn't hurt, either.) So one week later, I was allowed to go home. I still went to the hospital daily for therapies, but it felt so good to be mostly home.

CHAPTER 13

JESUS IN THE JUNKYARD

"**M**om!" John hollered toward the kitchen. "Mike is playing the guitar too loud again and I can't hear the TV!"

Knowing I was unlikely to get in trouble, I smiled to myself.

After living in a hospital for more than two months, being at home in that first-floor bedroom my family had arranged for me felt especially precious. Because I wasn't yet attending school, I continued to go to the hospital three times a week to receive my therapies. The rhythm of speech therapy, PT, and OT were a lot like they'd been for a few months, except that I got to come *home* afterwards.

Throughout my recovery, I'd been motivated to work hard for the youth group's fall retreat. Truly, I'd been willing to put up with wound scrubs and whatever other nonsense was required of me for the privilege of being sprung free the last weekend in October to join my Northview crew at the fall retreat to Kentucky Lake.

Although I wasn't in the regular habit of using a calendar, the retreat was scheduled in my mind for one week after my return home. I hoped I'd be ready.

Even I could admit that it would require much more of me than hobbling out of my wheelchair at home to sit at the dining room table for dinner. Though I understood that the terrain, schedule, and social atmosphere of Kentucky Lake might all prove to be overwhelming, I was desperate to join my peers for the final fall retreat of my high school experience. I held precious memories of Don leading worship at that retreat and then handing it over to me the previous year, and I was hungry to get back with those people, in that space, with that vibe.

On Friday, after other kids got out of school, mom and I joined two hundred other students on a few charter buses to the mountains. When we arrived, students and adult volunteers were more than happy to unload my wheelchair, help me into it, and drag our stuff to the room my mom and I would share. While I would have loved to have been in the big loud bunkroom with my buddies, I knew my physical needs precluded it. I was grateful just to be there.

It was amazing to see all the kids I'd missed over the previous two and a half months, and they were happy to see me. Even though my mom had to babysit me, I loved eating in the dining hall with Matt, Jason, Sam, and John. Other kids would stop by to let me know how glad they were that I was back. I'd usually say something socially appropriate, like "thanks" or "great to see you," but a few times my words got garbled. When that would happen, my mom would do her best to fill in the weird gaps in logic to make whatever I'd said feel slightly less awkward.

Because I was still a little drugged up, I knew I wasn't in any shape to lead the worship team. But I'd brought my guitar and when it was time to sing the final song, I was invited on stage. Several students had already mapped the route for my chair and helped me up.

"Thank you," I said as I settled in front of a microphone that had been lowered to my face level. "It's so great to be here. God is good."

Students began clapping praise to God.

While I typically would have prepared more purposefully to lead the room in worship, continuing to direct hearts toward Jesus, all I could spit out was, "Let's do this."

That was enough. The team launched into "God of Wonders" and—as if on autopilot—I was *all in*. My fingers knew the chords. My body felt the rhythm. And my mouth sang the words.

At the conclusion of a song, it's typical to wind down by repeating the chorus two times. Which, as the song leader, I did.

The problem, though, was that I repeated the chorus a third time. Everyone joined in, likely thinking I was particularly inspired to worship that night. But by the time I was bringing it around for the seventh time, it had gotten pretty weird. Don hopped up on stage, put his arm on my shoulder, and began praying, if only as a cue for me to bring it home.

I had an amazing weekend and couldn't stop gushing about it on the ride home. By the time we pulled into Carmel, I'd said all the words that were in me. When my dad met us at the door, I was roused enough to say "hi" and "goodnight." He helped me to the bathroom and into bed.

Before I fell asleep, I heard my mom telling him how great the weekend had been. She giggled a little when she reported some of the funny things I'd said to friends that came *close* to making sense, but really didn't.

My ramblings were easy enough to write off as the result of fatigue or the stressors of the trip. Both of those were easier to acknowledge than what might also have been going on in my brain at the time. We all knew that my brain had been injured ten weeks earlier, but no medical professional was ever able to say definitively how much I'd been impacted or to what degree I would recover. And so we pressed on, hoping for the best.

If the fall retreat had opened the door for me to rejoin the worship team, I was eager to walk—I mean "roll"—through it.

The following week I showed up early at the Barn to rehearse with the team before youth group. Wheeling up to the steps of the stage, I grabbed my crutches and hobbled up to the platform. When I plopped into the chair that was waiting for me, a girl on the team brought my guitar, the Phoenix, to me.

Don had been leading the worship band since my accident, and it felt good to see him up front. As practice unfolded, he suggested that he and I alternate leading songs and transitions. After having looped through seven consecutive choruses of "God of Wonders" the previous weekend, I thought it said a lot about his confidence in me that he was willing to let me anywhere *near* a microphone. For about twenty-five minutes of singing, we shared the responsibility for leading worship.

I knew I was still in recovery mode. My energy level was still pretty low and my ability to lead a group was still affected by the challenges I had putting all my words together because of the brain injury. I knew I was there to do what I could do, and that was to play and sing.

In the earliest days after my accident, I had been the recipient of the prayers of my community. When I was unconscious, when I was sleeping, when I was drugged up, when my brain was malfunctioning, when my body was broken, the faithful prayer warriors at Northview Church petitioned God on my behalf. Their faith sustained mine.

When I returned home from the hospital, though, especially before I returned to school, I had time and space to seek Jesus for myself. Until then, I had been the *object* of His love through all the miracles that had taken place in my healing to that point. But now I was searching for meaning. I wanted to know what Jesus was up to. There was no doubt in my mind that I'd been saved for a purpose, and I was eager to discover what that was. What is my part? What should I do next?

I didn't yet know, but I was eager to say yes.

When my mom and I returned from the retreat, I couldn't stop talking about it. While it had been hard on my body, it had been refreshing for my soul. After dinner I found my dad in the living room reading a book. I dropped onto the couch beside him, laying my crutches at my side.

"Hey, Dad," I said tentatively, "I've been thinking about something."

Looking up, he answered, "Sure, Mike, what's up?"

"Well, you know how there's a lot I don't remember about the accident, right?"

Nodding, he said, "Yeah, I know."

"I feel like there's still one big missing piece..."

"What's that?" he asked.

"I want to see the truck," I announced, not knowing how he'd react. The police had told us the truck had been towed to a local scrap metal yard.

My dad set his book down on the couch and thought it over.

"I think that's not a bad idea," he said finally. "Why don't we go when I finish at the office tomorrow?"

"Can Matt come?"

"Of course."

Later that night, as I drifted off to sleep, I tried to imagine the truck. I'd seen the video from police cameras, so I could visualize the *scene* of the accident. I listened in as investigators narrated where I'd lost control of the car, its untethered trajectory, and the point of impact. I'd visited the site with my parents, and we'd thanked God for His mercy and grace.

But I still needed to see my red Ford Ranger.

The one thing I did know was that my truck wasn't the one I'd known. It was no longer the trusted companion that had hauled me from yard to yard to make some money in the summer. It wasn't the friend that carried me home after a swim meet. It wasn't the helper that let me meet up with girls at O'Charleys. In a single moment, my friend had become my enemy. And at the scrap yard, I'd be facing down the archnemesis who tried to take me down to the grave.

I needed to be brave. And I needed to see it for myself.

■　　■　　■

So, two and a half months after impact, my dad, my brother John, Matt, John Murnane from my life group, and I visited the junkyard where my truck had been towed. My dad parked near the business office and dipped inside to ask for directions to the Ford. The wheelchair I used at school wouldn't make it over the unpaved ground, so I used my crutches to hobble to the site.

My right leg felt really heavy. I still had extremely poor circulation there, so as I navigated through smashed hoods, loose bumpers, and dented hub caps, I was keenly aware of my weighty extremity.

My brother was the first to spot the truck.

"There it is!" he said, pointing to a heap of metal under a nearby tree.

"Whoa!" John Murnane marveled. "It is destroyed."

The only person not surprised by the awful sight was Matt.

Though the truck was sandwiched between two other cars, we were able to move between them and survey its condition. Every inch of the exterior had been burned, and the front end had been crushed. Red cloth seats had been incinerated along with the rest of the interior. The subwoofer speaker I'd mowed nine lawns to pay for had been burnt up. Truly, nothing survived except me. Because the frame was crushed, I couldn't even imagine how Matt could have gotten the door open.

"Look at that!" I exclaimed, taking in the wreck. "That is amazing that it burned all this."

We marveled over the horrible wreckage. Dad was silent, and Matt quietly hummed to himself.

Pointing to the passenger seat, Matt suddenly exclaimed, "Dude, I know there was an angel right here. It's not like I saw him with my eyes, but I knew he was there. Helping."

I limped around the entire circumference of the vehicle, noticing the twisted metal, charred interior, and hollowed-out frame. The steering wheel, however, didn't look the way I'd remembered it. It was still wide, black, and circular, but in the fire, the center of it had melted the crosspieces that had previously been set at sixty-degree angles into the form of a crucifix.

"Look at this, Dad," I said. "This is so cool. There's a cross in the center of the steering wheel!"

Everyone peered in to see the steering wheel.

"Man, that's amazing," Matt said, awestruck. "Jesus was there, man."

My brother shot video of the wreckage, and after we'd fished out the burnt plug-in for my guitar from the back seat, we headed home.

After dinner, when I went to my room to do my homework, my mind kept wandering back to what I'd seen. In the days since my accident, my heart and mind had been humming, trying to process what I'd endured. On the most brutal days—when a saline wash was poured over my wounds, or when I'd wake up terrified that I was trapped in my truck—it was hard to find meaning in it. But that was the ongoing work of my heart and mind.

During the most difficult days in the hospital, I had been comforted by one thing: Christ had been with me in the fire and in the field. That was the solid ground that allowed me to make meaning of my suffering, to build a story that made sense. Matt had been aware of the clear presence of an angelic helper inside the truck. He'd witnessed Christ's bodily presence kneeling over me and offering the care and attention my body needed. And then the abundant love of Jesus continued to be poured out through His Body, showering my family with the provision, love, and support we needed.

When we trudged through the junkyard to see the truck, I'd been looking for more than charred remains. I'd been looking for meaning. I'd been looking for reassurance that I had not been alone in the fire.

I'd been looking for Jesus in the junkyard.

And I found Him there.

CHAPTER 14

DIVING BACK IN

"**M**om, hurry!" I shouted. "Let's go!"

"Well, look who's rushing who," she said playfully, as the person who was more often waiting on me.

Dr. Jones had cleared me to return to school the first week of November. But more importantly, he'd said I could go to swim practice because the chlorine was good for my burns. And the Friday before I'd return to attend school for half days, Mom was taking me to practice for the first time.

I was pumped to be back in the pool with the team, but I was also nervous. I knew that my cardiovascular endurance would be abysmal after being bedbound for almost three months. I'd been working on my flexibility in PT, being extra careful to stretch my tight Achilles. Because I'd lost thirty-eight pounds in the hospital, I knew my frame was thinner than when most of my friends had last seen me. Mostly, though, I was nervous about them seeing the burns and scars on my body. Whenever I'd had visitors in the hospital, including guys from the team, my wounds had always been covered by bandages, a sheet, or light clothing. But wearing only a Speedo suddenly felt even more vulnerable than usual. Would my teammates be repulsed? Would they look away? Would swimmers from other teams make fun of me?

We were running late after searching for my goggles, and by the time we got to the school's locker room at 2:40, the rest of the team was already in the pool.

"Mom," I said, standing from my wheelchair at the door to the locker room to receive the crutches she handed me, "I'm really nervous."

She knew why.

"They haven't seen my legs."

"I know," she said soothingly, "but I really think it's going to be fine. All of the guys love you and I don't think it will be an issue."

I wanted to believe her.

"I just know if I saw someone whose body looked like mine for the first time, I might be freaked out."

"I think you're thinking about it more than they will be, honey. Just enjoy being back in the pool."

"OK," I agreed reluctantly. "I'll try."

My gut told me that neither one of us was really convinced it would be fine.

Years later I'd learn that, after she left the school that morning, Mom cried the whole way home. She had prayed by my bedside; she'd fed me ice chips; she'd organized and administered all my meds; she'd facilitated all my care. But what she couldn't do was live in the ravaged body that was mine. While the busy pace of my care kept her mind occupied, my return to school meant that she'd finally have space to process all that had happened. And those tears of helplessness were part of that process.

Leaving my chair in the hallway, I hobbled into the locker room on my crutches, tossed my gym bag on a bench, and hung up my jacket. After undressing, I gingerly removed the dressings from the wounds that were still open, dropping them in a nearby trash can, knowing I'd need to redress the wounds after practice. Then I put on my swimsuit for the first time in three months. Quickly wrapping a towel around my waist and pulling my goggles over my head and around my neck, I shoved all my things into the locker. Grabbing my crutches, grateful the floor wasn't yet puddling with water, I made my way toward the pool, pausing as I passed a full-length mirror. Carefully opening the towel that was protecting me, I surveyed what my friends and coach would see when I got in the pool. Because the burns weren't fully healed, scar tissue hadn't yet formed, so the skin on my lower legs was red, raw, and partially scabbed.

Pushing through the swinging door to the pool deck, I quietly walked to the pool where the team was already swimming laps. After greeting Coach Busby and the trainers, I laid my crutches on the bleachers, removed my towel, and hung it over the bleacher railing for quick retrieval when I finished.

As I stepped toward the pool, a few swimmers on deck started clapping. As those in the water heard the slow applause, they paused from their workouts to join in. In moments, the room was thundering in celebration of my return to the pool. The reverberating echoes were pierced with a few shouts of "Kinney!" and "Welcome back!" and "We missed you!" Heart swelling in my chest, I suddenly didn't feel like the kid in a wheelchair, or the kid with a brain injury, or even the kid with the burns. I felt like a swimmer who'd gotten injured and was getting back in the water.

I'd be lying if I said that practice was easy. Not yet ready to dive into the pool, I carefully sat on the edge and slowly lowered myself into the water. I immediately felt the difference in the ways my legs and feet moved. While the rhythm and stretch of my kicks had always matched before, my body now moved unevenly. For the first several laps I kept a pretty slow pace as I tried to feel my way, encouraging my tight, compromised right ankle to match its counterpart. And, as expected, my endurance was weak.

At the end of my junior year, my times qualified me for the 400-yard relay at state finals. Although our team didn't place, I was confident that I could increase my workouts over the summer to improve my times. And if I could get my 500-yard freestyle down from 5:03 to 4:58, I could qualify to swim the event at the state championship meet.

That first day back in the pool confirmed my hunch that I wouldn't be breaking records my senior year. I wouldn't be earning points for my team. But I would be swimming. I'd be with my friends. I'd be normal.

When I walked out to the parking lot with my friends after practice, my mom was standing beside her car at the curb, talking to Coach Busby.

"So how'd it go?" she asked as I tossed my bag in the back seat and slid in to the front passenger seat. I could tell she was trying to be nonchalant, but I heard the concern in her voice.

"It was great," I reported. "I can tell I'm not as strong, but it felt awesome to be in the water."

"I'm so glad to hear that," she said. "Coach said you swam 3,600 yards?!"

"I did! Which kind of surprised me, too." I added, "I'm gonna sleep good tonight!"

"You sure will," she replied.

I stared out the window, replaying practice in my mind. After a few minutes, Mom interrupted my daydreams.

"Mike," she began, "I've really seen you mature this year."

"Thanks, Mom," I said, thinking she was probably right.

"I mean it," she said. "I'm amazed each day that passes at the new things He shows me. I know it hasn't been easy, but I'm amazed each day at how far you've come and how you continue to do your best with all of this."

"Wow, Mom," I said, "thanks."

I didn't *feel* a lot more mature than I had been three months earlier, but I wanted to believe she was right.

She added, "I wish my dad were alive to see all of this. He would've been so proud of you."

My grandfather had died before I was born, but Mom always said I would have loved him and that he would have really loved me.

"Awww…" I said, "Thanks, Mom. That means a lot."

She'd reported that her dad would be proud, but of course I also heard her letting me know that *she* was proud of me. Without flipping on the radio or starting a CD, we continued driving home in silence.

When my doctors had given me the green light to return to school at the beginning of November, Noblesville High had been in session about nine weeks. I'd be returning for half-days the first week, and then would attempt full days. Because of my lingering cognitive challenges, I was still scheduled to return to school as a student in the Special Ed department. And I'd be using a wheelchair. I felt like I was returning to school as a different person.

Will other students still see me as the old Mike?

Or will they pity me as broken Mike, and make fun of me in the hallways using hushed voices?

I expected that my season in the Special Ed program would be brief, and I was not looking forward to it. Those who learned differently were judged by kids like me as being *different*. Some spoke differently than most of their peers. Some had been born with Down syndrome. Others with more severe physical limitations, who used wheelchairs, also had intellectual challenges. Several used crutches with arm braces to help them walk. And of course there were students with learning challenges, like autism and other diagnoses, that couldn't be identified by facial features, adaptive equipment, or any other physical markers. But because they learned in Special Ed classrooms, even those who might otherwise slide under their peers' keen teen difference-seeking radar if they were sitting in a movie theater or coffee shop, were quietly labeled as "other." And I'm not talking about the mean boys who would mimic the limping gait of the one with cerebral palsy or the mean girls who'd text one another about the flamboyant fashion choices of a girl with Williams syndrome. I mean that even the "nice kids"—the kind that went to my church, the kind who were like me!—had a silent agreement that students who learned in the special ed classrooms were at the bottom of the social food chain. Even if "we" were nice to "them" at church, anyone with a choice would choose to be in the "we" group and not the "them" group. And although I had plans to graduate from special ed and go back into a regular classroom before the end of the semester, I couldn't afford to ignore the undeniable reality of the immutable adolescent social order.

On the first Monday in November, my mom hauled my wheelchair out of the trunk of the seven-passenger Ford van we affectionately called "Ol' Blue," popped the chair open, and dropped an extra pad across the seat. Using the car door and seat to support myself, I was able to rise to my feet, putting most of my weight on my left side, and pivot to sit back down in the chair. Butterflies fluttered in my gut.

My navy-blue backpack was hanging off the back of the chair as I balanced my crutches at my side. *Nothing weird about my mom pushing me into school in a wheelchair*, I thought quietly to myself. *It's pretty much the same thing as if the popular quarterback had busted up his knee.*

Even I didn't believe that one.

After stopping in the main office to confirm which classroom was mine, we wound through the halls on the main floor toward the elevator. Lots of students who normally wouldn't have even noticed me called out, "Hey, Mike! Welcome back!" Girls from the youth group would bend over to give me a hug and tell me how glad they were that I was back. (Now *that* I could get used to.)

When we entered the classroom where I'd spend first period, my mom propped my crutches up near the door and handed me my backpack before giving me a quick kiss and leaving.

Feeling uncomfortable, I had to remind myself why I was there: I was still having trouble accessing some words. When I told a story, it didn't always make sense. I was struggling to stay focused and organized. In the special ed classroom, I could receive extra assistance from the aids so I could graduate with my class in June.

Glancing around the room after my mom left, I noticed other students who had trouble using their words. I heard one boy using sentences that didn't make sense. Others were clearly struggling to stay focused and organized. Although I'd always believed that I was categorically different than the students I'd always seen getting off the short bus in the school parking lot, it was getting harder to convince myself that I was. The kids who surrounded me were actually a lot like the ones I'd been with in the hospital for the last two and a half months.

By the end of that first morning back to school, I was exhausted. When the rest of the class headed for the lunchroom, the aid who'd been helping me pushed my chair back through the hallways toward the front of the school, where Mom was waiting to drive me home.

In the crush of the main hallway, a few guys from the swim team were about to head off campus to grab lunch.

"Hey, Mike!" one said, "How you doing? How you feeling?"

It felt awkward that I had to look *up* at anyone who spoke to me.

"I'm doing good," I assured him with a smile. "I'm feeling a lot better, thanks, man."

As the guys swept past me and out the door to the student parking lot, I began to notice the way other students, and even teachers, looked at me. A girl on the swim team smiled awkwardly, waved, then pivoted away as if she didn't know what to say. A guy who'd gone to my elementary school breezed past and gave me a high five—but I'd seen the look of pity wash over his face. A freshman I'd seen at church caught up to walk beside us for a few steps, saying, "Hey Mike, my family and I have been praying for you."

"Thanks, bro," I answered. "I really appreciate it."

I did appreciate it, but the truth was that I'd have much preferred to be the magnanimous guy who was praying for the person who was sick, injured, or grieving than the *object* of others' well-meaning prayers.

In some ways, my stay in the hospital had prepared me for that first day. For weeks I'd been "the kid who had the accident." "The kid with the burns." "The kid in the chair." But being back in school took it to a whole other level. I was suddenly in the spotlight. Even students I'd never met knew me as "the kid who had the car wreck." That first week, I only wanted to be invisible. To fly under the radar. To blend in. But every look of pity I glimpsed on the faces of other students reminded me that I *wasn't* normal.

I wasn't.

Coach Busby saw me fighting through the crowds to get out of school and caught up with me.

"Kinney," he said, "it's great to have you back. Will we see you at practice today?"

"Yeah," I said excitedly. "I've gotta take a quick rest at home, but I'll be back for practice."

"Well, the team needs you, so I'm glad you're back."

"Thanks, Coach. Me, too."

He said, "I read that compression suits could help with your burns, and so I ordered you a sharkskin swimsuit like Olympic swimmers wear. I'll give it to you this afternoon."

I was touched by his kindness. While I knew that the suit wouldn't improve circulation or reduce pain like a compression stocking could, it would help protect the raw, open wounds on my legs and hide my burns.

"Thank you so much!"

"I want you to be really intentional about stretching before workouts, even if it takes some extra time, OK?"

"Yeah, of course, Coach. Will do."

Now it was official. I was back.

Although I wasn't ready to compete in the earliest meets of the season, six weeks after I first reentered the water, I competed against Ben Davis High School in the 100m freestyle.

Climbing onto the blocks at our team's home pool, wearing my black full-leg swimsuit, I felt the familiar pre-race butterflies in my gut.

After naming the competitors in the first seven lanes, the home announcer's voice bellowed, "In Lane Eight, from Noblesville, and coming back to the pool for the first time since his car accident, we are fortunate he is here with us today...Mike Kinney!"

Stepping up onto the blocks, I glanced toward the stands. Hundreds of fans rose to their feet and began clapping and cheering. As it had during my first practice, the aquatic center filled with joyful noise as my goggles pooled with tears. Quickly pulling them away from my face, I released the salty tears, wiped my cheeks, and tried to settle down.

That beautiful moment felt like a slow-motion scene from a movie. Stretching each arm behind my head, purposing to keep my emotions in check, I felt proud of how far I'd come since the accident and even optimistic that my recovery would continue. I knew I still faced challenges, but the amazing love and support I was receiving made me feel like I could overcome any obstacle.

As much to my surprise as anyone else's, I came in third place in my race.

I was getting stronger and reaching my goals.

CHAPTER 15

NOODLING ON WHAT'S NEXT

Where should I go to college?
What should I study?
What career should I pursue?

These were the kinds of questions my peers were asking during fall semester of our senior year. And at the time, I had no clear sense of leading or direction.

What I did have, however, was a quiet suspicion. While I didn't talk about it a lot with either family or friends, I had an inkling that God wanted me to continue leading worship as a bona fide professional. I'd had some good conversations with Don about what I needed to do in order to one day become a full-time worship leader in a church like Northview; I needed to do an internship that would give me more experience both in leading worship and in leading a team of musicians. I filed the information away, confident that God would open the door at the right time.

Because I'd started working on my college-application essays over the summer before my accident, my mom had been able to help me complete the applications in the hospital and after I returned home. I began to receive notices of acceptance at the end of the year.

In the middle of December, I was disappointed to receive a thin envelope from Purdue University informing me that my academic record did not meet the requirements necessary for admission. The school has a great reputation in Indiana, and a few of my friends were planning to go there. While I'd always known getting in would be a bit of a reach, the rejection was still disappointing.

Thankfully, three days later I received a thicker envelope announcing that I'd been accepted to Anderson University. Anderson, a private Christian liberal arts college, was a forty-five-minute drive from home. That meant I could be near doctors and family if I needed them, and I'd still have opportunities to continue to grow spiritually. From the moment I ripped open the letter, I was #TeamAndersonForLife.

The first Christmas morning following my accident was in some ways like a lot of other Kinney Christmases. My mom made an amazing brunch, and the five of us stayed in our pj's most of the day and exchanged gifts.

When it seemed as though we'd opened every last gift, my dad pulled a small box from a nearby bookshelf.

"We've got one more," he announced, "for Mike."

As he handed me the small gift box, he was clearly eager to see my reaction. Tearing the red-and-white-striped paper off and lifting the cardboard lid, I saw a thick gold ring that looked a little like one of the class rings being marketed to seniors—but it wasn't. Looking closely, I realized an image had been carved onto its broad face: a silhouette of a man emerging from fiery flames, with hands lifted to heaven. Running my fingers over it, I noticed an engraving on the inside of the band: "Used by God – 8/16/02."

"Mike, your dad sketched that image," Mom said, "and he's been so excited to give this to you."

"Dad," I said, feeling a bit awed, "it's amazing. Thank you."

"I got one for Matt, too!" Dad said. "We can go give it to him this afternoon."

"Is it the same as mine?"

"The words are the same," he said, "but the picture on Matt's ring is of him, hands raised, and head bowed in prayer, in front of a truck that's on fire."

"That's so cool, Dad," I said. "This is really, really special. Thank you."

Standing up from the couch, which still took some maneuvering for me, I stepped over ribbons and wrapping debris to give him a big hug.

"Mike, I thank God every day that you are alive, and I know that God has a purpose for your life," he told me.

My mind flashed to a letter stashed in my desk drawer that my dad had written me when I was twelve. Before my life ever took a dramatic twist, he had been convinced that God would use me, and said so in the letter he wrote to mark my transition into manhood.

While I didn't yet see the purpose my dad seemed to see, I wanted to. And the ring on my finger would be a constant reminder of it.

I quietly hoped that purpose was to lead worship.

One evening I was doing homework when my phone rang—a welcome interruption.

"Hey Mike, it's Don."

"Hey Don," I said. "What's up?"

"Well," he began, "I know you'll be at Anderson, but I was wondering if you'd be interested in doing an internship next fall and spring at Northview as a worship leader with the youth group."

"What?!" I exclaimed. "That would be awesome! What would I be doing?"

"You would be picking the set list each week and leading band rehearsals on Sunday afternoons before leading services on Sunday night."

"Totally!" I agreed. "That sounds awesome."

"I can only offer a stipend of $200 per month," he said.

Honestly, I would have been on board if he'd charged me to serve as an intern. And $200 a month to do what gave me life felt like a dream come true. Making the round trip once a week wouldn't be an issue.

"I can do it. I'm in!"

"That's great, Mike," he said. "We can talk more about it over the summer. I think this will be great for you and great for Northview. Thanks, man."

That was a total win for me! It was clearly the next step I needed to take in the journey to live out the purpose God had for me.

"Thanks, Don. I'm psyched about this. See you Sunday!"

"See you then," he replied.

I wanted to share the good news with the first person I found. I headed for the living room, calling, "Mom! Dad!"

"In here!" Mom yelled from the living room where she was finishing up a crossword puzzle.

I felt like I was sprinting toward her, but I was probably going at normal person's "walking" speed.

"Is Dad here?" I asked eagerly.

"No," she said, "he's at a meeting at church. What is it, Mike?"

"Don asked if I'd be a worship leader intern next year!"

She looked confused.

"While you're in school?" she asked.

"Yeah, I'd just drive home once a week. It's perfect!"

"Well," she said with a grin, "I wouldn't hate seeing you once a week." Then she added cautiously, "But I want to make sure it's not too much your first year of college."

Her concern didn't surprise me.

"Don't worry, I got it. I can totally do that."

As someone who struggled a bit to stay organized, and even more so since the accident, I wasn't completely sure I believed it myself. But the opportunity was too good to pass up.

"Well," Mom said, "if you can keep your grades up at school, it sounds like something you'd love and be great at."

"Right?!" I agreed. "Thanks, Mom. I'm super psyched.

"Go finish your homework," she said. "You need to pass this semester if you're even going to go to college. First things first."

"Totally," I agreed. "I'm almost done. Will you tell me when Dad gets home?"

"Sure, honey," she agreed.

I tried to get back to chemistry, but I was pretty distracted. I kept imagining Chris Tomlin leading worship and how awesome it would be to get to do that full time. My mom wasn't wrong, though. First, I had to graduate from high school. I resisted the urge to call Matt and stuck my nose back in the books.

That spring I tried to decide what my major would be at Anderson. Music performance made the most sense, but a business degree might also be a smart choice. I think it worried my dad that I couldn't tell him for sure what my major would be. He knew a career counselor, Dr. Faley, who performed an extensive inventory that helped both young people and adults determine the career that best suited them, and how to take steps toward it. My older sister Rachel had had a great experience with him, so I scheduled a time to meet with him, too.

In preparation for my appointment with Dr. Faley I took a thousand-question test, identifying interests, gifts, aptitudes, etc. And the day I visited his office, we had an extensive conversation that he recorded. I shared with him how much I enjoyed everything about leading worship at church: playing the guitar, singing, serving people, and helping them grow close to God. Having expressed my interests and desires, I was confident that he would be as helpful to me as he'd been to Rachel.

After our conversation we took a short break and then met again to discuss my results.

"You said you wanted to be a worship leader," Dr. Faley began, "but I'm going to tell you that you'd hate your life."

If my future had already felt hazy, in that moment it went dark. I struggled to even understand what he was saying—something about orchestral musicians, who made a living playing the oboe or violin or cello.

"These musicians who find satisfaction in a career like this are largely right-brained," he explained, "while you're more evenly split between right and left."

I knew that was true. I'm creative, but I also have a strong analytical side.

He said more things; I remember him citing the fact that I didn't read sheet music and didn't care to learn how.

After dashing the deep dream of my heart, Dr. Faley noted my high scores in marketing and sales. I was disappointed but trusted his expertise. Maybe he could see something that I couldn't?

I didn't realize at the time that there was something I could see that the good doctor could not. While I knew that being an orchestral musician and leading worship were apples and oranges—no, apples and cheeseburgers—I didn't challenge his pronouncement. Did he even know what leading worship was? A worship leader postures his or her worship to the glory of God, and directs others' attention to Him; an orchestral musician is a *performer*. I had no interest in being a showman.

But I didn't say that.

I simply assumed that he knew better than I did. And since my dad was absolutely convinced that Dr. Faley knew more than I did, he got on board the marketing train, encouraging me to start looking at Anderson's business course offerings.

I did, half-heartedly.

But the other half of my heart felt crushed that the dream that gave me life felt like it was dying.

One Saturday morning six months after the accident, the Red Cross inducted a cohort of local heroes who'd helped others. One was a police officer who'd taken a bullet while protecting civilians; another was a nurse who'd donated an organ to save a patient's life. And two more were my own personal heroes: Matt Blickendorf and John Kirby, the one motorist who had finally stopped to help Matt as all the others looked on.

My folks and I arrived a bit before the ceremony and were chatting with Matt's parents, Joni and Jim, when Matt turned to me, pointed to the end of the hallway, and said, "Mike, there's John Kirby."

John, who was sporting a white shirt and khaki pants, noticed Matt and headed in our direction. As he approached us, the blood seemed to drain from his face.

Dumbstruck, he could only choke out the words, "There's no way you're alive."

As he had come to be celebrated for my rescue, he *knew* that I had lived. But since we'd never seen or heard from him over the months I'd been recuperating, John Kirby was still envisioning my lifeless, battered body sprawled in a field.

Of course, I'd gotten pretty comfortable with the reality of surviving my accident, so his awe caught me off guard.

"Your legs were severed. Your chest was caved in. Your head was bashed in," he said, staring at me in shock.

Seeing how undone he was, part of me wanted to comfort him. Instead, I said simply, "Yeah, it was all so crazy. But here I am. Made it out of the hospital. I was in a wheelchair, but now I'm glad to be done with it."

He continued to look me over, up and down, as if to confirm that I was the same guy who had lain lifeless and broken in that soybean field. He was like Jesus's pal Thomas, who was wrestling to believe that his teacher and friend had been resurrected. Suddenly I could hear Thomas mumbling, "There's no way You're alive."

"Man," I said, shaking John's hand, "I can't thank you enough for stopping. For saving my life. Words don't even do it. I'm just so grateful."

At that moment a neatly dressed woman emerged from the auditorium to announce to the chatty crowd, "We're getting started!"

"Okay," Matt said, "let's do this!"

Leaving John, we rejoined our parents and found seats together in the middle of the auditorium, planting Matt on the end of the aisle. He and John were fifth in line to be recognized. When it was time to honor them, the emcee read a brief synopsis of their heroics before inviting them onstage to receive their awards.

"...and if it weren't for Matt Blickendorf and John Kirby," he bellowed, "Mike Kinney wouldn't be here today!"

The room erupted in applause.

Hustling to the front, receiving the microphone from the emcee, Matt delivered his brief acceptance speech and proceeded to share a thirty-second presentation of the Gospel. I noticed he was wearing the ring my dad had given him at Christmas on the hand wrapped around the mic.

When he offered the mic to John to say a few words, John declined. After the ceremony, he ducked quickly out of the event. It was the first and last time I'd ever see him.

I've always known and appreciated the fact that I survived my accident because of Matt. And yet because Matt had been unable to wrestle me out of the car using all his might, I truly do owe my life to the reluctantly brave John Kirby.

God uses who He uses.

The Red Cross event set me to thinking about my part in the story God was weaving. I believed I'd been saved for a purpose, but what it was I didn't yet know.

After sliding into the back seat of my mom's minivan after the ceremony, I buckled up and looked down at my right hand. Sliding off my own gold ring, I looked again at the words carved inside: "Used by God." But rather than feeling affirmed by them, my heart felt a little anxious. I knew how God had used Matt and John. But I was less clear on what it meant that God had used, or was using, me for His purposes.

"Does Outback sound good for lunch?" Mom asked, tipping her face back toward me.

"Yeah," I said, "it sounds awesome."

Thoughts of the blooming onion appetizer interrupted my reverie. But that question about how God would use me would continue to rattle around in my heart.

CHAPTER 16

REACHING KLANCY

One of the great joys of returning to the life I'd once known was leading worship each Sunday at the Barn. I loved planning for it. I loved rehearsing. I loved leading.

One night after youth group Matt and I were talking as I packed up my guitar when someone behind us said, "Hey, guys."

Turning, I saw it was Dan West—a longtime church acquaintance, but not a friend at school. I was surprised he'd approached us.

"Hey, man," Matt answered, "what's up?"

"I've been thinking about something," Dan said, "and I wanted to run it past you."

"Sure," I said, "shoot."

"Well," he began, glancing nervously at us, "I think you're supposed to share your story."

Matt and I exchanged glances. We'd been praying about how we could best share about what had happened in the soybean field.

"And," Dan continued, "I think I'm supposed to share mine."

Although I didn't know everything about Dan's story, I knew he'd been born with just two fingers on one hand, which he often hid in his pocket. And I'd also heard that he'd had some issues with drugs.

Having no idea what we were agreeing to, Matt and I said in unison, "Yeah! Let's do it!"

Later that week the three of us got together and imagined sharing our stories at an all-school assembly at Noblesville High. As Matt and I got to know Dan better, we learned more about how Christ had captured his heart and changed his life, and we started to get even more excited about what God wanted to do through us.

Three weeks later, with the permission of the school administrators, our dream became a reality.

On Tuesday morning I pressed through noontime cafeteria traffic wearing a black T-shirt with white lettering that said: "It only takes an instant to change a life forever."

"Hey, man," I called out to a buddy from youth group, pointing to my shirt, "it's happening today during fourth period, come to the auditorium."

Because we'd be sharing our faith, students couldn't be *required* to attend the assembly, but any student was welcome to come to hear us share about the accident. Matt and I were eager to tell students about the real Hero of the story in the soybean field.

We had no idea how many students would show up. Two weeks earlier I'd posted fliers around the school with a picture we'd taken when we visited the scrapyard of the truck's charred interior. There was also a photograph from a newspaper article of Matt visiting me in the hospital. The invitation on the flier was clear: "Come discover how the same Miracle that saved this soul can save yours."

Because I'd been given a pass to get out of third period, I arrived early to prepare for our presentation. As I entered through the back doors of the darkened room, I saw Matt and Dan sitting on the front of the stage, feet dangling.

"Hey, guys!" I called out through the silent space.

"Kinney!" they yelled, hopping off the stage and giving me a quick hug.

We reviewed our plan before bowing our heads and praying that God would be glorified through us.

We wanted for every student to hear that God loved them and had died for them. We knew that some of them were tripped up from believing in God because of bad things happening in the world and in their lives, so my encounter, a legitimate "bad thing," was an opportunity to testify to God's presence in the smoke and fire of our lives. And Dan's disability and newfound freedom from drug use would also testify to God's faithfulness.

After third period dismissed, students began trickling into the auditorium. By the time the bell signaling the start of fourth period rang, almost all six hundred seats on the first floor of the auditorium were full.

Nervous and excited, I welcomed the students before handing the mic over to Matt, who shared the narrative of the accident that I couldn't because I'd been unconscious for most of it. My experience of "the accident" really began in the hospital when I began to become aware of what was happening around me: when a screw was surgically implanted in the facial bones under my eye and my body began

to knit itself back together. When my grafting surgeries finally suc-
ceeded and my tissue slowly began to heal. How my brain began to
improve as I worked at my various therapies. How my community
had begged God to save and to heal me, and how we were now seeing
the fruit of their prayers and of God's faithfulness.

But what continued to niggle at my insides both while I was in the
hospital and after I returned home were those other pediatric patients
around me. The girl who'd flipped her car. The boy who'd been born
with an injured brain. An infant who'd been severely abused by his
parents who might never swim in a pool or flirt with a girl or play a
guitar. Like many who survive what others do not, especially as a
person of faith, I quietly wrestled with questions of God's sovereignty.
Why had I been saved? Why had others not? Though I didn't share
this ongoing turmoil with others, it continued to nag at my heart.

So when I came across an article in the *Indianapolis Star* by an
Episcopalian priest about how God is and is not involved in the
events of our lives, I was keenly attuned to look for answers to the
dilemma that swirled inside me. The piece was titled "God Isn't
Sovereign over All Events." And while at first it may sound like an
unlikely witness to God's goodness, the author's assertion that God
is not a divine orchestrator of events that turn out well for the
prosperous and poorly for the weak made sense to me. God is not
One who is absent in our suffering, but instead suffers with us. And
that's exactly what I wanted students to hear.

I didn't, and couldn't, know what every student's "burning
truck" looked like. What I did know was that they had suffered in
various ways, just as I had. I knew of one student at school who'd
survived cancer as a child. Another had lost her mom in a car accident. Someone else had battled an eating disorder. And even though

I wasn't personally aware of anyone who'd suffered physical or sexual abuse as a child, I knew that, statistically, there must be some among the students in my school.

On the night of my accident, God was not elsewhere. He was in the truck with me. And He was kneeling at my side, binding my wounds, in the smoky field after my rescue. He even showed up in the person of John Kirby, who refused to ignore my suffering. Everything in me wanted for students to know that—whatever they had suffered or would endure in the future—God was with them.

Dan then shared his story, and I could see students receiving the goodness he was offering by the expressions on their faces. After they filed out of the auditorium to get to their next classes, Matt and Dan and I gathered our things and I breathed a quiet prayer for God to touch the lives of those who needed to know His steadfast, faithful presence in their lives.

The rest of the week, I was flying high. Students I'd pass in the hallway would thank me for sharing my story, or friends from youth group would give me a high five. Matt and I had asked God for an opportunity to share about Him, and He'd answered that prayer.

The last period of the day, I had chemistry. That Friday, with only three weeks of school left, it was hard to stay focused. The weather was beautiful, and Matt and I were going to stay overnight at his family's lake house. I tried to listen to my teacher's lecture, but my eyes were glued to the minute hand on the clock over his head. While my teacher was saying something about molecules, I was mentally packing my duffel bag with what I'd take to the lake. After an eternity, the bell rang and I shoved everything from my desk into my backpack.

"Hey, Mike?" I heard a girl ask tentatively.

Klancy's desk faced mine. For the entire semester we'd been assigned to sit facing one another in a working-group cluster, but I didn't know her at all outside of the classroom.

"Yeah," I answered, "what's up?"

Whatever it was, I didn't want it to take long. I was meeting Matt at my house at three.

"Uhh..." she hedged, uncomfortably, "I just wanted to give you this."

Klancy held out a tightly folded piece of lined notebook paper with my name scribbled across the front.

"Hey, thanks," I said, searching her face for clues. *Should I open it? Should I save it for later?*

"OK," she said with relief. Before turning to join the other students pressing toward the door, she added, "I just wanted you to have that."

"Cool," I said, calling after her, "thanks."

Shoving the note in my pocket, I joined the other students hustling toward the parking lot.

When I got to my car—OK, my *mom's van*—I turned the key in the ignition and rolled down the windows. I was in a rush to get home and grab what I needed for the lake, but was curious about Klancy's note. *Is it going to say that she likes me? Is it going to say that a friend of hers likes me?*

Instead, it began, "Mike, I seriously want to thank you for yesterday..."

She was thanking me for our presentation. Without reading further, I jammed the note back in my pocket and backed up the van to join the line of cars full of other students eager to start the weekend. I'd read it later.

When Matt pulled into my driveway at 3 p.m. I was ready to roll. "Bye, Mom!" I yelled toward the kitchen. "See you tomorrow!"

"Have a good time," she called back. "Be safe!"

Scooping up my black-and-gold Purdue duffel bag I shut the door behind me and hopped into the passenger seat of Matt's car.

"Hey, man!" he greeted me.

"What's happening? I answered.

Matt began talking about how great it had felt to do the assembly together. Even though he didn't attend Noblesville, he said several students had stopped him afterward to thank him for what he'd shared.

Suddenly, I remembered the note from Klancy.

"Oh yeah," I said, pulling it out. "This girl in my chem class gave me a note…"

Unfolding it, I began to read it aloud.

Mike,
I seriously want to thank you for yesterday. You changed
my life completely. I've been through a lot lately—a
life-threatening moment of trying to kill myself.

"What?!" Matt exclaimed.

"Oh man," I said, as shocked as he was, "I didn't read the whole thing…"

I continued reading aloud,

After yesterday I realized that God saved me for a
reason. I didn't have faith in Him enough and I didn't

know enough. Last night I spoke to Him and asked Him
to come into my heart.

"Praise God!" Matt exclaimed.
I kept reading Klancy's words,

I owe it to you. I thanked God for saving you and sending
you to save me. Thank you so much for telling your story!
You're an amazing person! I love you for this and thank
you. I can't find the words to thank you enough.
Love Always, Klancy
I've never seen my mom cry so hard.
May God always be with you!

I was blown away. That note reflected exactly what Matt and I had asked God to do: touch the lives of students with His love.

Matt was pumped. But as he began talking rapidly about how many other students had also heard the message of salvation, my mind had gone someplace else. One sentence of Klancy's message had landed squarely in my heart: "I thanked God for saving you and sending you to save me."

What seemed so transparent to Klancy hadn't been as clear to me. All of the news reports had celebrated, even glorified, the heroism of Matt and John Kirby, and rightly so. Like six hundred other students at Noblesville High that week, I'd listened to Matt name the prime actors in my rescue as the helping angels and the kneeling Christ, and rightly so. In both narratives, however, I was little more than a charred victim. I was rescued, but I wasn't an *actor* in the story.

But Klancy's words reminded me that I was more than an object of assistance: God had saved me for a purpose, and part of that purpose was to touch the lives of others, like her and her mother.

I unzipped a pocket on my duffel bag and carefully placed Klancy's note inside for safekeeping. It would serve as a reminder to me that God had work for me to do.

Matt had turned on the radio, and as we drove, I kept thinking about Klancy. I didn't know how she had attempted to take her life. But for whatever reason, I pictured her by herself in a bathroom. Knowing nothing about the circumstances of her life or that moment, I imagined how desperately alone she must have felt in those hours or minutes of despair. But as I closed my eyes, I could suddenly see that she wasn't alone. While there wasn't another physical presence with her, I knew that God had been with her in that bathroom. She hadn't been alone after all. The same way God met me in the fire, I knew in my deep places that He had been with Klancy in hers.

A few weeks later, I received an award from my peers at the all-school assembly for being The Most Inspirational graduating senior. My parents had received a cryptic form-letter invitation from the principal inviting them to the ceremony, but no details were given. When I filed into the auditorium with my chemistry class, Mom had spotted me and waved. As I was climbing the six stairs to the stage to receive the award, I could see both my parents glowing with pride.

While someone else might have seen the award as a concluding acknowledgement, a period at the end of a sentence, it didn't feel that way to me: it felt like *expectation*. That eight-by-ten inch dark wooden plaque meant to me that my community expected big things from me. My parents expected big things. I expected big things.

I hoped I could deliver.

CHAPTER 17

THE MUSIC LIFE

Per Dr. Faley's expert advice, I enrolled at Anderson as a marketing major and planned to take elective courses in music. To be clear, marketing was just my major; my passion was still music. But I got to take some classes in which I learned about songwriting, music as a business, how people secured agency representation, and more.

Over the summer, my parents had replaced my truck. And when I say "replaced," I mean they'd found a replica of the red Ford Ranger that had gone up in smoke. Though it seemed a bit like a sick joke, I knew they were trying to help me. In the middle of August—one year after my accident—my parents and I caravanned to Anderson, where I shared a dorm room with a guy from Illinois.

While I mostly kept up in my classes, my real joy was being holed up in my room playing guitar and writing songs for up to six or seven hours a day. I was passionate about making a difference in the world through my music, and I was leaning into what I believed to be my purpose.

If I was fully dressed, I seemed like anyone else wandering around campus. And yet while other students couldn't always see my burns, I still lived with lingering effects of my accident. For instance, whenever I needed shoes, I had to buy two pairs. My left foot was a size nine, but since the accident my right foot had been a size ten. If the shoe on my right foot was even a little bit too tight, it would break open the skin on the outside of my ankle—which could lead to dangerous infections. When that would happen, my right leg would turn purple from my foot all the way up to my groin, swelling the lymph nodes in my groin. I'd be unable to take a single step without someone's help. It happened often enough after I started school that I started to get used to it, but it was always painful and scary. My body was telling me that I couldn't do what I used to be able to do, and I wasn't listening very well.

One day I was walking across the part of campus known as the "valley" when I felt the stab of a thousand knives in my groin. I knew the pain signaled infection, and I was suddenly unable to walk. A guy from my dorm noticed me, and I flagged him over. He helped me limp to the campus health center. By the time we arrived, I was in a cold sweat. After being treated, I limped back to my room alone.

The wintry Midwest weather didn't help my body. When temperatures dropped, the burn scars on my right leg would shrink, causing more pain than usual. Knowing the inherent risks of making even the simplest movements, like walking, I drove from class to class whenever possible. The parking spots I needed, those closest to the buildings, were designated for those with special needs. And yet as an eighteen-year-old college freshman, the very last thing I wanted was a sign on my car indicating that I was eligible to park in a handicapped space, so my ill-advised game plan was to park in the spots *without* ever applying for the designated sticker. Each time I got a ticket, which was often, I pulled it out from under my windshield wiper and stuck it in my glove compartment. Eventually I was no longer able to shut it because it was jammed full of parking tickets! So the next time I went home I pulled them all out and tucked them in a stack of mail at home for my parents to find.

I was limited by my injuries, but I didn't want to admit it. If I didn't have the sticker, I reasoned, then I didn't have a problem.

It was working for me.

To offset my academic load my second semester, I'd taken a lowkey water aerobics class to fulfill a P.E. requirement. While that may seem like a weak choice for someone who'd swum competitively, it really was the best one for my body.

When I pulled up to the school's athletic center on the first day of class, another student who drove an accessible van had snagged the closest parking space. Sliding into the second available spot, I grabbed my backpack, stepped out of the truck, and headed inside.

In the locker room, I noticed a guy using a wheelchair. He had burn scars over his entire face and head. And although he had no way of seeing what we had in common at that moment, I was keenly aware of what he must feel. When he changed out of his street clothes, I saw that most of his body was discolored from healed burns and skin grafts, too. The ways his body mirrored my own made me feel anxious, but I was curious.

"Hey man," I greeted him cheerfully before changing into my suit, "I'm Mike."

"Tony," he grunted, barely looking my way.

"Nice to meet you," I said.

He didn't answer.

"You live on campus?" I asked, suddenly realizing I'd never even noticed whether all the dorms had ramps or not.

"No" was his curt reply.

While I'd hoped to connect with him, the vibes Tony was sending clearly said, "Not interested," so I returned to where I'd dropped my bag and changed into my suit.

I couldn't help but remember a similar moment less than a year earlier. Being in a swimsuit with most of the skin on my body exposed again brought back the feelings I'd had the first time I returned to swim practice. I wish I could say I no longer struggled with fear over what people would think of my scars, but I was still very conscious of it. At that point in my recovery, the scar tissue was a darker red than the rest of my skin. Various areas of the scarred surface were depressed, shiny, and smooth, while others were noticeably raised due to inflammation. And when it was cold, they were purple.

But when I got on the pool deck, I was only thinking about the eyes of one classmate. As the teacher welcomed us and shared what we'd be doing during the semester, I noticed Tony looking at the mottled discoloration on my legs. I quietly hoped it might open a door for us to connect, but throughout the semester he seemed to make a point of ignoring me. I regret that I didn't push through the discomfort to pursue him.

That evening, I called my parents. When my mom picked up the phone, I started crying.

"Mike," she asked, "are you OK?" Then I heard her yell to my dad in another room, "Wayne, get on the phone."

I told them about Tony and how the experience had touched me so deeply. My extreme reaction wasn't a mystery: I was still figuring out how to live with burn scars myself. And while I wished I didn't care what others thought of me, I *did* care. And I was wrestling to figure out what it meant to be recognized as a burn survivor.

My parents listened well. "Mike," Mom said as we were hanging up, "I'm going to be praying for Tony and praying for you."

I knew she would be.

I learned later through other students that Tony had been burned badly as a child at home—and, heartbreakingly, it was *not* an accident. One of his parents had burned him intentionally. The act was unthinkable.

Although we were at a Christian college, I didn't know anything about Tony's faith. I didn't know if he'd wondered where God was when he was suffering. I didn't know if he'd ever encountered the Father of Jesus, who is *good*. I prayed that he had, but the way I saw his cool interactions with others on campus signaled that he may not have known either the steadfast, unfailing love of a human parent or a divine one.

GOD'S PRESENCE IN THE FIRE

Although I had experienced God's presence with me in my fire, many have not in theirs. That's not to say that God wasn't there. But for a variety of reasons, many who suffer struggle to believe that God is with them and for them. The college student who was raped on campus naturally wonders where God was as she was being assaulted. The father of a four-year-old who died from cancer naturally wonders where a loving God was when his child died. The wife of a young man critically injured by a drunk driver who left him permanently brain injured naturally wonders where God was at the moment of impact.

If God is good, how can He allow the kind of human suffering that so many endure?

I don't presume to have a simple answer for why God allows evil. I'd be suspicious of anyone who did. But I do carry these beloved sufferers in my heart. I long for them to know in their deep places the steadfast love of a faithful God who sees them and hears them and knows them and loves them. And I am convinced that a gracious God who longs to be known is not limited by time and space. That means that someone who has lived for eighty years under the crippling weight of a childhood hurt can ask God to show her where Jesus was in that moment. It means that even if we felt abandoned in our most terrifying experiences, the Holy Spirt can open the eyes and ears of our hearts to see Jesus's face and hear His voice in the moments when we were unaware of His presence with us.

It's what I pray for Tony. And if you have not yet known Jesus's intimate presence with you in the flames you've endured, it's what I pray for you.

One of the highlights of my first year at Anderson was playing in a band called Unusual Mix with three other guys. School had been out a few weeks and a few of us were hanging out in a practice room in the school's music department, where I was working on composing a song called "Bigger Than Me," using two capos on my guitar.

A capo is a device that can be clamped onto the neck of either an acoustic or electric guitar to raise the pitch by shortening the strings, providing "vibration termination." Most often, a capo would be fastened across all six strings of the guitar, which we sometimes refer to as "full capos"; these help performers easily change the key of any song without changing his chord finger positions. Partial capos that apply pressure to only a certain number of strings are also available in pre-set configurations that cannot be modified; these allow the guitarist to create new tuning possibilities. A full capo can be clamped onto the neck of the guitar behind a partial as well. Although they're used most often in styles like blues, flamenco, and folk music, many rock and pop players—including Tom Petty, John Mayer, and Bruce Springsteen—have used capos.

As I was fiddling with the new melodies, our lead guitarist teased, "Why don't you learn how to play without the capos, Kinney?"

His implication, which I heard loud and clear, was that using a capo was "cheating." While capos can make learning easier for beginning guitarists, they also allow for more nuanced sounds from advanced players. So I ignored him.

In May, I drove home to celebrate my birthday with my family. Mom made her scrumptious lasagna for dinner as well as a double chocolate cake with nineteen candles on top. During the meal I learned that my parents had spoken to Jim and Pat Sorum, who were once again concerned about Jamie. Her life and her relationship with her boyfriend, Jasen, were going well. But she was tripping and falling a lot, which seemed weird. And sometimes she had trouble getting her words out, which of course I could relate to. Pat thought Jamie's struggles could be related to the antidepressant her doctor had prescribed; they were going to have some tests done to learn more. Rachel gave me a T-shirt emblazoned with the logo of my favorite band, Coldplay, John gave me a book of coupons for a car wash, and my parents gave me a gift certificate to Guitar Center. After dinner, John and I played video games until I went to bed a bit after ten. I was still in the downstairs room that had been converted from an office after my accident.

Three hours later I bolted upright in my bed. My bedside clocked glowed 1:19 a.m. Before I awoke, I had been on stage in a grand auditorium, playing the guitar in front of thousands of people, using a new kind of capo for guitars that I knew did not yet exist outside of my dream. That moment of awakening—literally and figuratively—pulsed with promise, and I knew instinctively that I needed to capture it before it faded from my awareness. I had been shown a new way to capo a guitar, and I felt like I'd been handed an amazing gift.

I stepped to my desk and turned on an old computer that took forever to power up. I willed my mind to stay in the zone so I could capture what I'd experienced in the dream.

When I was finally able to create a document, I started typing as fast as I could. What I really needed was design software to execute what I saw in my mind, but in lieu of that I used the underscore key to type a line across the width of the page. Then I created spaces using the delete key to indicate frets and began to count how many ways a musician could capo one of the frets.

The capo I envisioned would offer sixty-three different ways to clamp any given fret (the space between the vertical strips, called fret bars, you see on the neck of a guitar). The top of the capo looked like an old cassette player with multiple buttons that could be pushed down individually or simultaneously like "Play," "Record," and "Pause." The bottom view looked like a typical rubber capo pad beneath the capo bar, except that it was broken into six sections (or feet) that would apply pressure to one or more of the selected strings.

As I pictured the capo attached to a guitar, the top of the capo bar was raised above certain strings and there were square rubber pads coming out of the bottom of the capo bar applying pressure to the other strings. It was easy to imagine the value a selectable partial capo would bring: It would make the guitar more like a piano because more octaves could easily be played all at once.

As I tapped away on the old computer, capturing everything I'd received in the dream, I felt a strong sense of God's presence and leading. In the hospital, I hadn't been able to lower my middle finger when instructed to do so. And now I'd been given a fresh way to help musicians, both beginners and seasoned players, do something they couldn't do before.

For example, let's say a guitarist recovering from a brain injury needs four chords for a song. With the new capo I'd been inspired to create, he could play those four chords with *one finger*! It simplified the chord structure, making it easier to play alternate forms.

In some ways the concept was simple, but Dad always said that simplicity is the ultimate sophistication. And while beginning guitarists could learn to play with one- and two-finger chord positions, more advanced players would have endless ways to play and create new sounds. It would give them a way to get out of their theory box and expand their horizons so the melody could take them places they might not have gone on their own.

The vision captured my heart, mind, and imagination. Two years earlier, Klancy had said in her note to me that God had saved me for a purpose. I already knew for certain that part of that purpose was to share His love with people like her. But in the wake of the dream, I was reminded again that another part was to reach people with music. And now God was helping me do that.

The next morning, I spilled out the entire vision to my parents over breakfast. They were happy for me, but I could see on their faces that they were weighing how excited they should be. Would this be a short-lived project? Would my enthusiasm waver? I knew I'd had a holy encounter that was intimately connected to God's purpose for me, and I understood it might take them a minute for them to get onboard.

For the next six months I researched everything there is to know about capos. I read every book or magazine article I could get my hands on. I used the new-ish search engine called "Google" to hunt for information. I ordered one from a brand called Third Hand Capo to test its capabilities, but it was pulling strings out of tune.

Like any other parents, mine didn't want me to be hurt or disappointed, and I understood that. But in that season of their ambivalence, I yearned for my dad, in particular, to believe in the capo like I did. And if I'm honest, his reservations about it touched on a more tender spot in my heart. I thought I wanted him to believe in the dream because that's easier to say than that I wanted him to believe in *me*—but that's really the thing for which I most hungered. In subtle ways—whether his remarks or his silence—I picked up on hints that my dad didn't believe I was as capable as I'd been before the accident. And although I did have new challenges, I wanted and needed the father I so admired to believe in me. I knew he loved me. I knew he was on my side. But I still yearned for him to believe that I was still the Mike who could do anything.

Gradually, as my folks saw my commitment, they got on board. Dad wanted to help me create a prototype of the capo I'd seen in the dream. So we started with a Kyser capo, cut the top bar off, replaced it with the one from the Third Hand capo, and wired it all together with dental acrylic from my dad's office. Some of the construction choices I was making didn't make sense to my dad's engineering brain, but I knew exactly what I'd seen in the dream and held fast to that vision.

That I had dreamed this on my birthday felt significant. I believe that each one of us on earth has a unique purpose, and this felt like it was part of mine. I literally felt like I'd been born for it.

This was the beginning of a journey that would continue to unfold for years to come.

CHAPTER 18

NOT AGAIN!

R ight before my sophomore year of college, we marked the second anniversary of my accident. At dinner the night before, Dad prayed for me, thanking God for protecting me and sparing my life. The next day, I hopped in my second red Ford Ranger to go pick up some needed strings at the Guitar Center. While driving I noticed I was feeling more tired than usual. As I zipped along Hazel Dell Road, I felt my eyelids begin to grow heavy. Raising my eyebrows, I purposed to keep my weary eyes open. Anyone traveling past me would also have seen me slapping myself in the face in an earnest attempt to stay awake! I made a mental note to start getting to bed earlier before school started the following week.

Moments later, my eyes opened and I realized I'd drifted off to sleep while traveling at fifty-five miles per hour. I saw the red flash of the brake lights of the blue sedan in front of me, and instinctively knew I wouldn't be able to slow down in time to avoid a collision. I swerved to the right and hit its side.

Fortunately, neither of us spun out or flipped off the road, and we were each able to steer our cars to the shoulder of the road and slow to a stop. With my heart racing, I turned off my engine and got out of my truck. The other driver, who appeared to be in his forties, was exiting his vehicle and gripping the back of his neck. *Was he injured?* Circling his car, he beelined for the damaged rear side panel. When he turned to look at me, I saw a flash of anger in his eyes.

I joined him and surveyed the damage. I was already sobbing. "I'm so sorry. I don't know what happened..."

The man seemed to soften in the face of my despair.

"We've gotta call the police," he said, intuitively understanding he'd need to take charge of the situation, "and then we'll exchange information."

"Yeah," I agreed, wiping the back of my hand across my face, trying to pull myself together. "I'm gonna call my parents."

I dreaded telling my parents what I'd done. Again. When I heard my mom's voice, I started crying again.

"Mom," I wept into my flip phone, "I just had an accident. What's wrong with me?!"

"Mike," she said calmly, "are you hurt? Where are you?"

"I'm OK," I said, "but this other guy might be injured. I'm on Hazel Dell just past 106th Street. Can you or Dad come?"

"Of course. Your dad's at work, but I'll be right there."

"OK, bye."

I rifled through my glove compartment, grabbed my crumpled insurance card, and returned to the side of the sedan.

"The police are on their way," the other driver said.

"I'm so sorry," I apologized again as he clutched his neck. "I had a car accident two years ago today. I actually almost died. So this is a crazy day for this to happen. I don't know what's wrong with me. I'm so sorry."

The driver compassionately listened as the story spilled out of me. Ten or fifteen minutes later, Mom pulled up just as a police officer slowed to a stop and got out of his car.

"Mom," I began, "I'm so sorry."

"Mike," she assured me, putting her arm around my shoulder and giving me a squeeze, "we're going to look into it and figure it out."

After the officer took a report and we exchanged insurance information with the other driver, a tow truck came to drag my Ranger away and I rode home with Mom. A mechanic called the next day to let us know that the frame had been bent and the extent of the repairs that would be needed to fix the truck.

My mom spent Tuesday morning on the phone, making arrangements for me to see a specialist who could diagnose whatever my problem was. The following week my dad took me to a sleep disorder center. After an initial interview, a nurse hooked me up to various wires to conduct a daytime sleep study. My instructions were to take a nap every two hours. That I could do.

Dad and I returned two weeks later to receive the results. We sat in twin wooden chairs across from his desk as the doctor explained, "You're not getting enough deep REM sleep."

"So," I asked, assuming the problem was my fault, "is that because I'm a college student and I'm supposed to be sleeping more?"

"Actually," he said, "it's more than that. You have a mild-to-moderate case of narcolepsy."

"Narcolepsy?" Dad asked.

"What's that?" I wondered aloud.

"Mike," the doctor said, "narcolepsy is a sleep disorder that can make you really sleepy during the daytime. And patients can have a sudden sleep attack at any time they're awake—"

I began to put the pieces together.

"Wait," I interrupted. "So that narco-whatever is why I had my first accident?!"

"Most likely," the doctor confirmed, nodding. "Because your body isn't getting the rest it needs at night, it tries to compensate by those sudden sleep attacks."

I thought of the cartoons I'd seen of someone going about their daily life when suddenly their eyes flap shut and they fall over sideways and start snoring. *Am I that guy?*

"I don't know why we didn't consider this possibility," Dad said, as if he could have saved me from either accident.

"It's not easy to spot, and a lot of people don't become aware of the condition until they have an adverse event like the ones you've experienced," the doctor said.

"So how is it treated?" Dad asked.

"There are daytime medications to stimulate the central nervous system to help keep patients awake," the doctor said. He wrote a prescription before we left the office.

On the drive home, more of the pieces of the narcolepsy puzzle began to fill my mind.

When I'd been at college the previous year, some of my friends had teased me for being spacey. In the dining hall or the dorm lounge my eyes would be open and I'd appear to be completely awake, and yet I noticed that I missed a lot of information. Only when someone asked me a question would I snap back to reality.

"What were you saying?" I'd ask, having missed most of the conversation.

I'd felt like something was off, but because I couldn't figure out what it was, being "spacey" just became my normal.

Whether I was listening to a teacher, watching a video for class, listening to a sermon or a guest lecturer, I was constantly scribbling down notes. While I presented as someone who was hungry for knowledge, and I certainly believed that I was, I was unwittingly working really hard to stay focused enough to retain information for which I'd be responsible. But when I studied with friends for tests, we noticed that my class notes would often be missing large sections of teaching. In group projects, I always felt like the weakest link.

Once, when I'd driven from Anderson to Calvin College in Grand Rapids, Michigan, to attend a concert, I'd snapped pictures the entire drive. I had photos of scenic views, of exit signs, of semi-tractor trailers, of golden arches, and even of roadkill along the highway. Just after crossing the state line, I noticed a couple of kids close to my age in a car alongside mine smiling at me. The driver gave me the "peace" sign with his fingers and the other pantomimed snapping a picture. Apparently they'd been watching me take photos for miles and wanted to star in one of them! After I obliged, they sped off, satisfied. I'd always assumed my endless pictures of nature meant that I just really liked the great outdoors, but I was beginning to realize I'd been compensating for my sleep disorder in ways I hadn't even been aware of for a long time.

The doctor had told us that narcolepsy usually doesn't develop until around the age of sixteen. I was definitely tired and depleted when I was sixteen, but assumed it was because I was swimming five hours a day! I ate a lot of nutrient-dense foods—and also Wendy's burgers—to replenish the energy I was expending by swimming.

When we got home, Dad and I sat down with Mom at the kitchen table to explain what we'd learned.

"How did we not see it?" she asked.

"It's not your fault, Mom," I assured her. "I don't think it was obvious." I shared the insights I'd been having about the ways I'd been compensating for the previous few years. "They said it might take some adjustments to get the right dose of medication," I explained. "But when it's working, it should help me stay awake."

"Yep," she said, "we'll keep at it until the dose is just right."

Although I sensed that my parents blamed themselves for not catching my narcolepsy sooner, my first accident and recovery had convinced me that I had two of the fiercest advocates a young man could ask for.

Accepting my diagnosis would be an ongoing process. On one hand, it was the long-awaited explanation for why I'd had my first accident. First responders had conducted routine testing for drug and alcohol use, and of course found nothing. So the only story we could piece together was that I'd been working hard, swimming hard, and not getting enough sleep. For years, a small part of me had felt guilty, believing that if I'd done something differently the accident wouldn't have happened. But the ways I'd compensated over the last two years suddenly made sense. The first accident hadn't been my fault, and neither was the second.

But as welcome as that insight was, I also felt like it was another challenge I had to manage. I'd learned how I could best use my body in ways that didn't aggravate my damaged skin. I was still discovering creative ways to compensate for my brain injury. And now *this*? It felt like just one more way I was broken.

Shortly afterward, my band, Unusual Mix, was playing at a gig for Oranghaus Records, a local label that had signed us to produce an album. After the show, I met a fellow Anderson student, a girl named Shelly. She was creative, which I loved, and committed to her faith. We began dating, and I grew more attached throughout the school year. During the spring semester she'd hang out with us at band practice as Unusual Mix prepared to spend the summer leading worship at a series of camps.

A few weeks before we went on tour, I opened the door to my dorm room and found a sealed white envelope with my name on it. Sitting down on my bed, I opened it. It was from Shelly. And she was breaking up with me.

She said a lot of the typical things that the person who breaks up says: *You're a really great guy; I care about you; I value our friendship.* Those were the opening act for the main event:

> *Based on a number of things I see in you, I don't know if we're compatible. You don't get to classes on time. You're not turning in your homework. These things concern me. And because you're not responsible, I question our relationship. I don't think it's going to work out.*

What?! She is breaking up with me?! Well that doesn't seem fair. Those things are just me. They're who I am. What can I even do about them?

I fell back onto my bed, glad my roommate was out, as tears forced their way out from behind my eyes. Thinking about some of the things Shelly had mentioned, I knew she wasn't wrong. It was true, I did struggle with a lot of those things.

What is wrong with me? Will I ever be enough for someone, or am I just chronically broken?

I feared the latter.

Two weeks later, when we left to begin visiting summer camps, my heart was still heavy as I grieved the loss of the girl I loved. Throughout the eight-week tour, nights and mornings were particularly difficult for me. About the only times I wasn't thinking about Shelly were when we were onstage, leading worship and singing our original songs.

That summer, the privilege of leading worship was God's gift to me.

Two years later, I graduated from Anderson with a degree in marketing. After all, that was what the vocational specialist had recommended.

CHAPTER 19

CHECKING ALL THE BOXES

"I'm a head hunter with Eagle Recruiting," said a deep-voiced man on the other end of the phone.

Is this really happening?

The words seemed too good to be true. My first job out of college had been at Campbell's Soup Company in Camden, New Jersey, and I'd just been fired after one year. I'd struggled to do well in the marketing department and was feeling like a failure after being let go. I had no idea what I'd do next.

Over the year I spent in New Jersey, I often measured myself and my performance against that of my team members in the marketing department. When I saw the ways a few of them were just so very well suited to their job, the ways that I was not felt particularly glaring.

Part of that failure was simply that I wasn't wired for that kind of work. Despite the pronouncement of the vocational wizard who had assured me I was made for marketing during my senior year of high school, the truth was that it hadn't been a good match with my natural gifts. But there was more.

After about six months in New Jersey, I met with Dr. Karl Doghramji, the medical director at Jefferson Sleep Disorders Center. In my initial interview I shared about both my car accidents, my narcolepsy, and the trouble I had with focus and daytime fatigue. I even confessed that I would sometimes fall asleep at red lights. Following a three-hour behavioral interview, Dr. D discovered that my initial diagnosis may have been incorrect. Rather than the "mild to moderate" case of narcolepsy I'd been told I had, his findings pointed to a "severe" case. In response, he tripled the dosage of medication I'd been taking to stay alert during the daytime, which worked wonders.

Dr. D also referred me to a specialist who conducted further neuropsychological testing. This doctor concluded that it didn't seem that the deficits we were seeing could easily be attributed only to my narcolepsy; he said my brain might not have recovered from the car accident as fully as we'd thought, since I'd experienced brain hemorrhaging. He believed I would continue to experience the kinds of mild anxiety and depression I'd had that year in New Jersey, which would exacerbate those cognitive weaknesses and "interfere with his most successful performance" in any job. That is the polite way of saying I was unlikely to succeed professionally. I chose not to linger on that opinion too long. While the specialist may have been right, and likely was, no good would come of me dwelling on it.

After being fired from Campbell's, I was driving my truck with all of my belongings over the Ben Franklin Bridge through Philadelphia, heading back to Indiana, when I received a call from an unidentified number. That was when the trajectory of my dismal professional life changed completely.

"Hello?" I said, picking up.

The voice on the other end announced, "I'm calling for Mike Kinney."

"This is Mike."

"Hi Mike," the man replied, "I'm Don Harrison and I'm a headhunter with Eagle Recruiting. I came across your resume and it seems like you'd be a perfect fit for a company I'm working with in Noblesville."

He had just named the town, still two states away, toward which I was driving. I was blown away by what I refused to believe was a coincidence. He told me more about the job—a marketing projects manager that required skills I'd gained at Campbell's Soup Company—and I shared how crazy it was that in that very moment I was leaving the job I'd had in New Jersey and was driving to Noblesville. We chatted for a while, and then Don asked if he could pray for me.

What? What business recruiters even do that?!

"Sure," I said, "that would be awesome."

Keeping my phone on speaker and my eyes on the road, I listened as Don prayed for me.

"God, we know you have a purpose for Mike and a plan for his life," he said. "You know exactly the steps laid out in front of him. We trust that You want the best for him, and together we pray that You would guide his steps going forward as he leaves this chapter of his life. We ask You to go in front of him and let him know You're with him."

Those words meant more to me than the one praying them could even have imagined.

When I'd started at Campbell's Soup, I'd had a powerful sense of God leading me there. So when I was let go, I was asking God if I'd even heard Him at all. But Don's prayer reminded me that God had been with me when I'd driven east over the Ben Franklin Bridge a year earlier, and He was with me that day as I headed west with my tail between my legs. God would be with me in the future He had in store for me.

It felt like the first of many holy encounters that I call "rainbow moments." While the skies on Interstate 70 between Pennsylvania and Indiana were sunny, with neither cloud nor rainbow in sight, it was the kind of moment of confirmation that God offered to Noah. I could hear God's quiet whisper assuring my heart, *I remember you, Mike, and I am faithful to you. This is a sign to remind you of my steadfast love and faithfulness, even when storm clouds hover.*

God had been present with me through a corporate recruiter named Don Harrison. It was a technique I'd seen Him use in the past, and one that I'd continue to recognize in the future: God brought a person into my life at just the right time to let me know that He was with me.

If that affirmation sounds familiar, it's because it's what I'd experienced in the fire as well. Jesus was present with me in the flames, and He was promising to remain with me when skies looked stormy.

My stormy skies had just brightened.

Though I'd only been working in Camden for a year, I'd lost part of myself there. I'd abandoned the Christ-centered boy I had been, getting lost in the party scene and a series of bad dating relationships. Although I couldn't have put my finger on it at the time, I was hurting emotionally. While I'd received a lot of love growing up, I didn't feel as capable or lovable after the accident, and I longed to fill those empty spaces. I desperately wanted to live up to the potential my dad saw in me when I was twelve years old. Not surprisingly, I suppose, I imagined that returning home to Indiana would help me find myself.

I saw returning home as an opportunity to reengage with music ministry. Although I'd visited various churches in New Jersey, I never joined one and certainly didn't get involved in leading music. I was hungry to once again use the gifts God had given me to serve His Body, and I was excited to connect with Northview's music pastor about joining the worship team.

After interviewing for the position for which the headhunter had contacted me, I was hired by Trails End, a Weaver Popcorn company. My job was to help the company transition from popcorn in metal tins—the kinds that Boy Scouts and other nonprofits peddle for fundraisers—to selling popcorn in standup, resealable pouches.

Because I didn't have the kind of intimate community of people around me in New Jersey that I'd had at Anderson and in Noblesville, I felt free to do what I wanted. One of those things was dating a woman who wasn't a Christian. I'd never felt quite right about the relationship, and I ended it because I knew it wasn't right for me. On my drive back to Indiana, I had begun to imagine meeting and dating a woman who was committed to her faith in Christ.

My return home promised to check all my boxes: music, career, and relationship. I joined the worship band at church. Check. I worked for a boss who believed in me and my gifts. Check. And not long after returning home I started dating a young woman, Katrina, who was working as an intern in the music department at Northview. Check.

But the reality of my new life was more complex than the neatly checked boxes.

I did love making music with the worship team. Northview had even begun to hire a few professional musicians who I'd played with in our college band, Unusual Mix. But even though I loved playing alongside those guys again, I found myself comparing my natural musical talent to theirs. Typically, no good comes from comparison, and that was absolutely the case for me. Beyond my own self-critique of my abilities, my brain injury was making learning new music tricky. I think it's also fair to say I could have been a stronger team player. Bottom line: I wasn't growing into the kind of worship ministry leader I'd always imagined I'd be. Although it wasn't what I expected, it was a season for self-reflection and growth.

On a brighter musical note, my dream for the capo was slowly moving forward. I had opportunities to talk to various developers and learned more about what was needed to successfully patent, market, and launch a new product. The dream that had been given to me years earlier continued to simmer inside me.

Like music, my work life also turned out to be trickier than I imagined. Even though I had a boss who believed in me and my gifts, I reached the end of the trail at Trails End after just two years, when the company reorganized. Then I started selling Crocs at the mall. And while selling brightly colored rubber shoes might not sound particularly glamorous, the job highlighted some of the unique strengths God had given me that I hadn't been using before. I loved connecting with people and discovered I was good at selling. I got to start conversations with customers about what they were looking for, whether they were buying for someone else, or if they'd worn Crocs before, and those conversations led to sales. In fact, some of the younger sales associates would laugh about how many pairs of shoes customers were buying from me each day. (The customer who bought eleven pairs will confirm that my technique of highlighting all the different occasions for which one would need a different pair of Crocs was effective!) God was starting to show me the ways I'd been uniquely designed to thrive professionally. I'd eventually leave that job and take a few more swings in sales and real estate before nestling into the thing for which I was most suited.

But at that time, my relationship with Katrina wasn't exactly flourishing. Throughout the course of our relationship, I knew in my deep places that she wasn't "the one." In fact, over the four years we dated, we broke up four times! I ignored what should have been a series of red flags because what we had was comfortable-ish. Although neither of us wanted to admit it, the relationship wasn't healthy or strong. Looking back, I can see that I was looking for my identity in another person, which had been a pattern in my dating relationships through college and beyond. If I wasn't in a relationship, I was hunting for the next one. In our third year of dating, Katrina and I were "on a break" when a friend of mine set me up on a blind date.

Jana and I had talked a bit on the phone the week after our mutual friend suggested we meet, and on Saturday I went over to the house she shared with a few friends to hang out. It was already pretty hot at the end of April, and I was wearing a white button-down shirt and navy shorts.

I rang the doorbell and waited, taking a deep breath for confidence.

A girl with long dark hair and big brown eyes opened the door. She was dressed in a pink T-shirt and denim shorts, and she seemed friendly enough.

"Hi, Jana?" I asked, confirming it was her. "I'm Mike, it's nice to meet you."

"Hey," she said with a smile, "nice to meet you. Come on in."

I felt a little anxious, like anyone might when meeting a stranger, but our conversations had been easy, and I had no reason to believe our visit wouldn't be as well. Stepping into the foyer, Jana pointed through a dining room toward a living room, where I could hear a tennis match on television. "You can go in there," she said.

She followed behind me at a bit of a distance. I sat down on the green floral couch but rather than joining me, or at least splitting the difference, she sat down on the opposite end. Since we'd hit it off over the phone, her coolness surprised me.

"Do you play?" I asked.

"What?!" she asked, sounding distracted and a bit perturbed.

"Do you play tennis?" I asked, hoping to connect.

She replied abruptly, "No."

As I looked toward the screen to see who was playing and what the score was, I felt her eyes on me. Tipping my head toward her, I saw her looking at the scars on my legs with horror. And then I heard her start gagging.

Is this really happening?

Before I could think of how to respond, Jana hopped up and ran to the bathroom.

Really?

I might expect a middle school boy to be rude enough to dry heave at something he found distasteful, but her behavior shocked me. And of course, it stung.

I walked straight back toward the front door, ready to leave. Although I'm still not sure why I thought I owed her the courtesy, I waited until she came out of the bathroom to let her know I was leaving.

"This is over," I announced. Opening the screen door, I turned and told her, "You need to grow up and handle things with a little more maturity. Because that's not how you treat people."

Letting the spring-loaded door slam shut behind me, I turned and walked back to my car. My insides felt like they wanted to cry, but I wouldn't allow them. This—being rejected by a girl because of my scars from the accident—was what I'd feared in the weeks after the accident when I saw what looked, to my eye, to be monstrous. But I'd had other relationships in college in which my scars hadn't even been an issue. I'd let my guard down, and Jana's behavior really took me by surprise.

What I'd said to her was true, but vague.

She did need to handle "things" differently. But in this case, "things" meant me. She hadn't disliked and mocked my car or my outfit. She'd been repulsed by *me*. She'd been cruel to *me*.

I took a few deep breaths as I got into my car and started the engine. I couldn't remember the last time I'd felt ashamed of my scars, and in that instant, I could think of nothing else. I could see nothing else. I could feel nothing else. The deep fear of my heart—that girls wouldn't find me attractive because of my scars—had been realized in the most bitterly painful way. And the fears that I'd tamped down for years bubbled up to the surface and overwhelmed me.

Closing my eyes before pulling away, I remembered the kind nurse in purple scrubs six and a half years earlier who'd revealed to me that she also lived with scars. I recalled that she'd identified them as battle wounds. They reminded her that she was strong. And brave. They reminded her that she'd survived.

I willed myself to channel her courage.

The battle was over. I'd won. And I wasn't about to let someone who'd likely never set foot on the battlefield rob me of my peace.

But still, Jana's actions stung.

When that nurse-soldier had been cleaning my wounds in the hospital, I could not have imagined the way my journey would have unfolded. If I'd been given a magic wand at that time to trace the trajectory of my perfect life going forward, I wouldn't have struggled to succeed in music ministry. I wouldn't have been fired—and then let go again. I wouldn't have spent four years in a relationship in which no one was flourishing. And I wouldn't have carried with me the battle scars I bore on my body.

Yet, in the midst of a life I couldn't or wouldn't have predicted, I still believed that God was leading me. And in that season, I witnessed a vibrant God-trusting resilience from a friend who was weathering her own fiery flames.

CHAPTER 20

JAMIE'S BURNING TRUCK

Long after the fun slumber parties of our youth, the Sorum family would still stay at my parents' home when they visited Indiana.

About five years after I finished college, the Sorums came so Jim could join Northview's summer mission trip to Nicaragua. He continued to nurture the relationships he'd developed over his years at the church and served when he could. So Pat, Jamie, and Jacob stayed with us while Jim was in Central America.

My mom, who'd left nursing after twenty-five years to help my dad run his dental practice, was at work when she got a call from home. It was John, who'd graduated from college a year earlier and was in nursing school. He was at home, visiting with his girlfriend, Morgan, during the Sorums' visit.

"Mom," John began, "something's weird here."

"Weird?" she asked. "What do you mean, 'weird'?"

"Morgan and I were watching TV and Jamie was in the kitchen. We heard her dropping dishes and it just seems like something's not right."

Mom paused, trying to decide what to do.

"Is Pat there?" she finally asked.

"She went to lunch with a friend. But I can talk to her when she gets back."

"I think that's a good idea," Mom said. "You can just share what you noticed and let her decide what to do."

"OK, thanks," John said before hanging up.

Twenty minutes later, Pat returned from her ladies' lunch, greeting John and Morgan in the living room.

Muting the television, John asked, "Pat?" Knowing Jamie was upstairs, he lowered his voice. "When Jamie was in the kitchen, it sounded like she was dropping plates and bowls and stuff. I don't know why, but it just seemed like something was wrong."

Pat asked, "Did you mention it to Jamie?"

"Uhh…" John hedged. "I didn't. I just didn't know what to do."

John knew Jamie had faced a variety of emotional challenges and wasn't sure whether he should get involved.

"I understand," Pat said. "We think the medication she's taking for her mood is having these undesirable side effects. We're going to talk to her doctor about it. Thanks for your concern, though, John. We appreciate it."

"Sure," John answered with relief. "I hope everything's OK."

When they returned to South Dakota, the Sorums mentioned Jamie's symptoms to her doctor at her next appointment—the clumsiness she'd experienced, her trouble articulating some words, and a scary fall down the stairs to their basement. The doctor assured them that the symptoms weren't related to the antidepressant and encouraged them to get further testing.

As soon as he spoke the words, Pat made a connection she hadn't thought about for years: Jamie had been adopted as an infant and, as with most closed adoptions, they only had a very limited amount of information about her birth parents. But Pat had an inkling that they could learn more if they could access Jamie's adoption records that had been sealed by the state of Indiana.

So the Sorums hired an attorney to petition the judge to open the sealed records. Those documents showed that Jamie's birth mother had had a brain disease called Huntington's chorea. There is no cure, and it is known for being brutal and relentlessly progressive.

Throughout our young adult years, Jamie and I had stayed in touch occasionally by text. Sometimes I'd let her know if I was dating someone. She'd let me know if she had broken up with a jerk or a great guy. We'd both marvel at how many weddings my sister Rachel was in.

One of the ways in which we often connected was by sharing the unique challenges we faced. It was comforting to have that friend who'd known you forever and would love you no matter what. I'd told her about my narcolepsy and the lingering effects of my brain injury. I knew that she had struggled with cutting and other emotional issues. Being honest about my brokenness always felt safe with Jamie.

Did I mention that Jamie was funny? Once she complained, "Well, my parents are always broke and everything in their kitchen

are gifts from their wedding and are so old and rotting and defec-
tive, including the knives. So when I would try to cut myself all
those years, every time I would do it, the blades on the knives were
so dull that they would just scrape and not cut! That is something
that would only happen to me."

That Jamie could take something so bitterly painful and find
lightness and levity in it was exactly who she was. Once, when she
was letting me know that her boyfriend of four years had broken
up with her, she grumped, "I am the one with bipolar, but his mood
swings were worse than mine."

That Jamie has always been easy to love.

Not long after that visit to Indiana, Jamie texted to let me know
she'd discovered the identity of her birth mother. She also shared
about her mother's condition and that she, herself, had been diagnosed with Huntington's. Though she didn't bemoan to me how
cruel the disease was, a quick online search revealed that it ravaged
the bodies of its hosts. Jamie told me that not only did her biological
mother suffer from Huntington's, but her biological grandmother
had died from it at age forty-five.

"Eleven years ago I was misdiagnosed with bipolar," she added.
"I learned that this happens quite frequently because Huntington's
is a brain disease and it affects people psychologically, physically,
and cognitively. It mimics the bipolar symptoms and causes severe
ups and downs."

The same way narcolepsy explained a lot of what had been
confusing for me, Jamie's unwelcome diagnosis explained many of
her earlier mental health issues.

She also told me that while the average life span after diagnosis
was fifteen years, she'd likely had it since she was sixteen. She was

now twenty-seven, and the doctor had given her ten more years to live. I couldn't even wrap my mind around receiving a death sentence like that. In predictably positive fashion, Jamie also said in the same breath that she was excited to meet her birth mother.

Jamie's incredible resilience shone through when she wrote, "I am incredibly sick, but I am ready. I wake up every morning and smile to have another day. Whether I have ten years or a lifetime left, I could not be more grateful. God has boosted me up to the top of the list, and I'll get to see Heaven earlier. I am ready when my time comes, and God always has a plan for me."

That last bit took my breath away. It's not that I don't believe it. I do. Ever since my accident I'd been convinced both that I had a special purpose and that God had a plan for everyone He'd created. What floored me was that Jamie could see that, could say that, in the midst of the chaos her life had become. So many who find themselves trapped in a fiery inferno are blinded by the smoky haze that surrounds them. But not Jamie. In the midst of the flames, she could see God's gracious hand in her life. In her story—a story that ultimately would glorify Him.

I struggled to know how to respond to Jamie's text. I expressed my concern. I let her know there was no way I could really understand. I assured her that I'd be praying for her.

"More specifically," I wrote, "I'll be praying that God gives you His strength and His peace as you prepare to meet your birth mom and that He would comfort you and your family as well as your birth mom and her family. I love you. Mike."

The Sorums located Jamie's birth mother, Angie, in an assisted living facility where she'd resided for the last seven years. Jamie was thrilled to learn that she had biological siblings. Sadly, most had also been diagnosed with Huntington's, including Jamie's eighteen-year-old half-sister—but because that sister had had the opportunity to start preventive medications at age fifteen, she was still fairly healthy.

Just a year later, however, when the Sorums visited Angie on their next visit to Indiana, the reality of what lay in store for Jamie was revealed. Angie had no control over her limbs. She wore a helmet to protect her during falls and the shaking that accompanied Huntington's Chorea. Staff had to feed and diaper her. The visit was sobering for the whole family.

But even after seeing what was ahead, Jamie wasn't rattled. She held her head high and, against all odds, she kept smiling.

When I'd last visited with Jamie in Indiana, she seemed so…normal. The antidepressant had helped her mood, and she was happy with her boyfriend, Jasen, who seemed like a really great guy. But after she was diagnosed, Mom told me Jamie broke off her relationship with Jasen so that he could have a life she couldn't offer him. At first he refused to break up, but eventually—reluctantly—he received her selfless gift.

After Jamie was diagnosed, the symptoms that she'd been "managing" began to worsen. Her speech became increasingly unclear, until friends and visitors could no longer understand her words. When she was no longer able to walk safely, she began using a wheelchair. And when she wasn't able to feed or relieve herself, her parents began performing the bulk of her daily care. Jamie was slowly being imprisoned in a body over which she had no control.

I thought about Jamie often. And while I could relate to the unintelligible speech, the wheelchair, and people bathing me and helping me go to the toilet, I was keenly aware that while my physical health largely improved, Jamie's future was dismal. After being rescued from the flames, my injuries and burns began to heal. With the exception of the lingering effects from my brain injury, and the limited flexibility stemming from the loss of elasticity in my burned skin and tendons, my trajectory was always toward recovery. Jamie's would be a steady decline in function until the grave.

Jamie had faith in Jesus during that season of discovery, but I couldn't imagine what that would look like after her diagnosis and in the days and years to come. Would she know the nearness of God's presence in her suffering? I prayed that she would.

CHAPTER 21

SURVIVING THE SMOKY SEASON

"Hey, man," my coworker asked, "what's up with that?"

In my job as a professional clothier, selling suits and sports coats to executives who were still required to wear them in their workplaces, a colleague pulled me aside to speak privately as we were getting into our cars after a client left.

I heard annoyance in his voice.

"What's up with *what*?" I asked.

"Mr. Stephenson tried to shake your hand and you left him hanging," he reported.

"Really?" I asked. "I honestly didn't catch that."

"I know," he said. "And it's not the first time, either."

What? This was hard to hear. Because my brain injury made it hard for me to keep track of tasks and to-do lists, I had always counted on my people skills to carry me at work.

177

"Gosh, man," I said, "I really don't know what's going on. That shouldn't be happening. I'll try to pay more attention."

Even as I said it, I knew that "attention" wasn't my strong suit. When I joined my family for Sunday dinner later that week, I told them what had happened.

"That doesn't sound like you," Mom said.

"I know, right?"

"You know what?" Dad said. "A patient of mine told me about a service called LearningRx. Apparently it's a national chain of centers that help people with brain challenges retrain their brains after an injury."

"But we don't even know if this is related to my accident," I pointed out.

"No, we don't," he agreed. "But it couldn't hurt to get an evaluation to see if they think they can help."

"I think it's a great idea," Mom said. "What do you think, Mike?"

The thought of more therapies bummed me out, but I didn't know what else to do. "I'll give it a try."

"Great," Mom said. "Hopefully we'll learn something useful."

Honestly not knowing what to expect, I felt weird walking into the LearningRx building at a nearby strip mall for my first appointment the following week. It had been eleven years since the accident, and I was frustrated to still be dealing with fallout from it.

After checking in at the front desk I fiddled with my phone until a therapist came into the waiting room.

"Michael Kinney?" she called out.

"Yup," I said, rising from my chair, "and you can call me Mike."

I had completed some brain exercises and testing before the appointment; one of the goals of our first meeting was to go over the results, which confirmed I had more complications from my injury than I knew.

Mom and I listened to the brain therapist, Kelly, share my prognosis.

"Mike, your visual processing speed is at the fourth percentile," she reported. "We think we can help you with that through our LearningRx program and one-on-one brain training activities. They are designed to focus on your areas of weakness and the areas of your brain that were injured." She proceeded to tell me that I had impaired facial recognition, spatial reasoning, and sequencing issues.

Somewhat in shock, I tried to wrap my damaged brain around the number she had shared. Being at the fourth percentile meant that ninety-six percent of my peers were visually processing things faster than me—and this had been going on for more than ten years.

Kelly waved her hand to regain my attention.

"We can also use the areas of your brain that are strong to help us rewire and retrain the areas that are weak."

When I arrived for my second appointment, Kelly met me and led me to a different office toward the back of the building. Now there was no turning back. Ready or not, it was time for me to face my limitations head on—no pun intended.

The office felt like a little living room; Kelly invited me to sit down in a chair facing hers and asked what had led me to make the appointment.

I told her about my accident, and the narcolepsy that was diagnosed a couple years later. I explained that because of the brain injury there were daily things I struggled to remember, but I had put systems in place to make sure I didn't forget important facts and appointments. I was as thorough as I could be, hoping she'd pick up on some kind of clue from my narrative. And then I explained the most recent motivation.

"At work and at church," I told her, "I've been missing handshakes. Like someone will extend their arm to shake my hand and I totally miss it. It's really embarrassing."

"Alright," she began, full of confidence, "Here's what I want you to do: I want you to tell me everything that you see behind me."

I couldn't figure out what was challenging about the simple exercise.

"Do I have to look and then close my eyes or something?" I asked, remembering some of the cognitive testing I'd undergone in the hospital.

"Nope," Kelly assured me, "it's easier than that. Just tell me what you see behind me."

It really was as easy as it sounded.

"OK," I said, "ready?"

She assured me, "I'm ready."

Feeling like I was really going to impress her, I started listing everything I saw: "Clock, book, magazine, framed picture, light switch, light, window, wall…"

I included "wall" just to let her know how thorough I was being.

When I was finished, she asked, "That's everything you see?"

"Yes, everything," I confirmed.

Flipping her chair around, Kelly dragged it in my direction and sat down beside me. She pointed to an electrical socket about eighteen inches above the floor and asked, "Did you see this?"

Surprised, I admitted, "No."

"And what about this?" she asked.

Following her arm, I saw a gray metal trash can with a plastic liner.

"I didn't notice that," I answered.

"Let's go higher," Kelly suggested. "What about these flowers?" She pointed at a small coffee table with a fresh bouquet of daisies on it.

"Gosh, I really didn't see it," I confessed.

I wasn't yet putting the pieces together, but I could tell that the clues meant something to Kelly. Turning her chair back to face me, she said, "I'd like for you to make an appointment with an ophthalmologist to get your eyesight checked."

I suddenly realized I couldn't remember the last time I'd seen an eye doctor.

"OK," I agreed, "I can do that."

"After you get your eyes checked, come back to see me."

Thanking her, I left the office. As I walked to my car, I couldn't help but wonder what was wrong with my eyesight. When I passed a parked U-Haul trailer, I could read the words on the back end. I could read the name of a restaurant on a tall sign across the street. And when I looked down the road a few more hundred yards, I could read that a gallon of gas cost $3.53. My vision seemed fine.

Dutifully, though, I visited the eye doctor a few weeks later. After examining me, his report was more shocking than the price of gas.

"Mike," he explained, "you have a significant loss in your field of vision."

"What does that mean?" I asked.

"Well," he said, pointing across the room, "imagine that I drew a large circle on the wall—"

"OK," I agreed.

"—and then I drew a horizontal line through the center of the circle—" he continued.

"Yeah...?" I asked, not knowing where he was going.

"Mike," he explained solemnly, "you're not seeing anything below that horizon line."

I saw a snapshot of Kelly's office in my mind, remembering that every object I'd identified had been up high, and I'd missed everything below the middle of the wall.

"So that's why I'm missing handshakes?" I said, for myself as much as for the doctor. "I can't see them?"

"Yes," he said, "that's likely exactly what's happening."

"But," I protested, "my accident was *twelve years ago*! Did this just start happening or something?"

"I don't think so," the doctor said. "What happens after a traumatic brain injury is that the rest of the body compensates, so you likely didn't even notice what you were missing."

I suddenly remembered the difference between the notes I was taking from the whiteboard in college being different from my classmates'. The doctor continued, "You've probably been making all kinds of adjustments to compensate for the loss."

"So," I wondered aloud, "am I like half-blind without even knowing it?"

He laughed.

"Well, you're not blind, because your eyes can see. But there are therapies and exercises you can do to retrain your brain that will likely increase your field of vision."

"Oh!" I said. "Yes! That's exactly how I got here. I went to a brain training center and the therapist suggested I get my eyes checked."

"That's great," he said. "Good luck."

He proceeded to give me multiple exercises I could do each day to help me improve my field of vision. I wondered how much of my visual processing speed had been impacted by that and how much of it was related to the brain injury. Regardless, I hoped that LearningRx could help me figure it out and make improvements.

As soon as I was back in my car, I called my mom to tell her what I'd learned.

"Isn't that crazy?!" I said. "For twelve years I didn't even notice."

"Oh, Mike," she replied, "I'm so sorry we didn't notice and get you the help you needed." The sadness in her voice echoed with the same regret I had heard when I was diagnosed with narcolepsy.

"It's not your fault," I assured her. "I'm the one who should have known."

"No," she said, "you were working to recover in so many areas. I just wish we'd caught it."

"Well," I offered, "we know now, so I can work on it. Hey, I've got to go, but be sure to tell Dad."

"I will, honey," she promised. "Thanks for calling."

"Love you, bye."

My mom had told me that early on in the hospital, my doctors had warned there could be ongoing issues as a result of the brain injury. But in those early days and weeks my parents had other priorities. Initially, they simply prayed that I would live. When I lived, they became concerned about saving my leg and making sure the burns would heal. Hoping that time would continue to heal my brain, they'd later admit they hadn't *wanted* to know more about the limitations I was facing. Like any other parents, they were looking to see "the old Mike." And as I slowly recovered, they saw what they were looking for.

I don't fault them for it. They just didn't notice New Mike.

After twelve weeks of intense therapy, I regained my full field of vision and made significant improvements in the areas of my brain that had been damaged in the accident. God had given me a good gift in the opportunity to get help and healing at LearningRx. Truly, it was a game changer for me. It helped me to stop second-guessing everything I did and accept that it was okay to make mistakes. When I did, I purposed to learn from them, move on, and try not to make the same ones again. When I stopped fighting the brain injury and committed myself to finding new solutions, I began to experience healing and freedom.

Standing alongside eight- and ten-year-olds at my LearningRx graduation—which, if I'm honest, still sort of makes me laugh—I was grateful that I'd been given the tools I needed to move forward.

My anthem song is how I experienced God's presence in the fiery flames. But I also think it's important to name the ways that He is present with us after we've been rescued. When the air is still smoky, when we don't yet have our bearings, when life is still not back to "normal"—*and may never be*—God is with us in the haze.

During the years after my accident, the consecutive "reveals" of my ongoing limitations just kept coming. And yet God was no less present with me through those than He was in the flames. He was with me as a Good Provider when I finally received the correct dosage of the right medicine for my narcolepsy. He was with me as the Author of creative solutions, quickening my mind to come up with ways to work around the limits I faced due to my brain injury—even when I wasn't aware I was doing it. And He was with me and all the other grade-school kids at LearningRx, as the Good Physician to help forge new neural pathways and restore what we'd lost.

God's presence in the trying seasons of our lives will look all kinds of ways. When the mother of a child trapped under an automobile accesses superhuman strength to lift it off, God is with her. When an angel shows up to inspire and comfort a teenager trying to rescue his friend, God is with him. And when a twenty-something guy is trying just to stay awake, function, and see normally, God is with him.

God is with *me*.

And God is with *you*.

CHAPTER 22

AN INTERESTING FELLA

The unkind words of the young woman who was repulsed by my scars made me wonder if there would be more women who would be disgusted by my body. In retrospect, it's no surprise that in the wake of that hurtful encounter I slid right back into the familiarity of my relationship with Katrina.

People who loved me, though, saw the toll that was taking on me. My friend Scott, with whom I was living at the time, was one of them. He'd watched me throughout my relationship with Katrina and consistently cautioned me against it.

We were smacking a ping-pong ball back and forth across the green table in Scott's basement one Saturday morning when he raised the issue again. The moment was right because Katrina was visiting her grandparents out of state. Had she been in town, she and I would have been together. Enmeshed. Going through the motions. Codependency kept us both locked in a relationship in which neither of us were flourishing. Though I didn't admit it, even to myself, I wanted *out*.

"Mike," Scott began, "you're not even yourself anymore. You've gotta end things with Katrina."

Nothing he said was new.

"But what would I tell her?" I asked him. "It's not like I can give her a good reason."

We both knew I'd tried to break it off several times before and had been unsuccessful.

"But you don't *owe* her anything," he said.

I knew he was right, but I still felt a profound sense of obligation. Katrina and I were both in our late twenties and had watched many of our friends marry and even begin to have children.

"Brother," Scott continued, "God's had His hand on your life the whole time. You're going to be fine."

An hour later, Katrina and I were arguing on the phone, and I broke up with her. It wasn't the first time, but it was the last time.

Though I probably shouldn't have let him, Scott had created a profile for me on Match.com once when Katrina and I had been on one of our "breaks." The afternoon I finally ended things with her, I opened Match on my phone and peeked at my account. There was a message waiting for me from someone named Liz. It read, simply, "You seem like an interesting fella."

I was intrigued.

Something about her profile really captured my heart. One of the pictures she'd posted—showing her at a wedding holding her friend's toddler—caught my attention. The little dude was wearing a cute little black vest over his starched white shirt, and Liz was wearing a flowing pale pink dress. It was easy for me to imagine that she'd be a loving mother. Her highlighted brown hair was swept up into a twist, with flowing wisps framing her face. She was beautiful. She seemed kind. She loved God. I wanted to know more.

After trading a few messages, Liz shared her number and I called her. After fifteen minutes, I'd learned that we had a lot in common. After four hours, I knew I had to meet this girl. Immediately.

The sky was white with snow and there was a winter weather advisory, cautioning travelers to stay at home. With a bit of sane reluctance—on Liz's part, not mine—we agreed to meet in the middle at the salon she managed, called Gentspa. Scott, clearly a wiser soul than I, begged me to heed the travel warnings. Headstrong and driven, I wasn't changing my mind. So my kind friend packed me a kit for the road: extra layers of clothes, blankets, windshield defrost, flares, and snacks for when I inevitably got stuck in weather thirty degrees below zero.

Leaving Noblesville to drive toward downtown Indianapolis, continuing to chat with Liz the whole way, I gripped the steering wheel as my windshield wipers fought to keep the glass clear. Skimming across frozen streets in my black Hyundai Sonata, I saw more than half a dozen cars slide off the road and down steep embankments. I mentioned none of them to Liz.

I've gotta meet this girl was the driving mantra pounding in my heart and head.

My Sonata actually lost all traction as I tried to climb the entrance ramp to the freeway. I was stuck. Not wanting to worry Liz—or discourage her from arriving at our meeting point—I simply announced, "Umm…I gotta go," before abruptly hanging up.

Glancing nervously at the clock on my dashboard, I knew there was no way I'd make it downtown by 7:45 p.m., when we'd agreed to meet. Nothing I tried would stop my wheels from spinning, and because police were ticketing any drivers foolish enough to ignore the weather advisory, it was fifteen minutes before another vehicle even approached the ramp. Soon, though, several semi-tractor trailers eager to get to their destinations were halted behind me. The drivers of all those vehicles were pretty motivated to see me move. About six big guys were finally able to dislodge me from the rut my tires had spun and quickly help me up the incline, where they pushed me onto the open road packed with snow.

Creeping along I-465 and then getting on I-70, going no faster than thirty miles per hour, I finally made it into the city and found parking near Chase Tower, just across Monument Circle from the Hilton Hotel. By that time it was after 9 p.m. The good news was that most Hoosiers had heeded the winter weather warning and wisely stayed home, so parking was simple! Grabbing my guitar, I tromped through fallen snow and into the hotel. Then I followed signs to Gentspa, which offered manicures, pedicures, and massages to men and women.

Liz spotted me as I was stomping the snow off my boots on the small rug outside the door. Smiling and waving at me, she unlocked the door and let me in. Everyone else had gone home, so we had the place to ourselves. Setting my guitar down at the reception desk, I peeled off my wet, snowy layers and sat down in the waiting area.

We picked up our conversation where we'd left off, and talked liked we'd known one another forever.

"What's your favorite worship song?" I asked her.

"Gosh, that's hard…" she admitted. "Mmm…maybe 'Here I Am to Worship?'"

"Cool," I said, and hopped up to grab my guitar. Clicking open the case, I pulled out the Phoenix and began strumming.

At the moment when vocalists would join the instruments, Liz began singing. I joined her on the second verse. We both felt comfortable with one another and, before we knew it, hours had just melted away.

This is crazy. This is happening.

We talked about everything from our siblings to my capo to our faith journeys and even my accident. We laughed over the fact that she had found me on Match.com after searching for keywords "Christian" and "guitarist." When I shared vulnerably about moral failings I'd had in previous romantic relationships, she listened well and had more grace for me than I had for myself. And she was honest and vulnerable about her own shortcomings. In fact, over the course of our conversation, I learned that Liz was separated and heading toward divorce. *How did I miss that on the dating profile?* I must have been blinded by her beauty. And although I knew that her divorce was imminent, it still gave me pause. I wanted, and we wanted, to do things right.

Before we parted later that night, I suggested that we not hang out again until her divorce papers were signed. Liz agreed.

I knew things were looking good for me when she skipped a day of work that week to knock out the final paperwork, get the signature of the man soon to be officially her "ex," and hand-deliver the documents to the courthouse.

For the four years since I'd returned from New Jersey, I'd been seeking my purpose. Was it music? Was it connected to the string of jobs I'd worked? Would it involve a woman with whom I'd share my life? On that very first weird, risky date with Liz, I wasn't asking any of those questions. Something inside me knew I had found someone who quieted my heart and who, in some weird way, felt like the *answer* to some of those questions. But it wasn't in the same way that I'd hoped some of the other girls I'd dated would be the "answer" to what I was seeking. Instead, I was genuinely interested in getting to know who she was and to share with her who I was. I felt...different.

Would I advise someone in a similar situation to give themselves time to heal from a previous relationship? I would. And yet, I wouldn't change a thing about the beginning of our story. I'd love it if each of us had had time to heal from our previous relationships, but I can also see the ways that offering one another acceptance and grace was an important part of the healing process we each were experiencing as our relationship blossomed.

The little seed that was planted on the night of January 5 took root in good soil. By the beginning of July, I knew I wanted to propose to Liz.

When I made my decision on July 11, I called a friend of Liz's who is a jeweler. By the end of the next day, he'd crafted for her the ring I described over the phone.

That night, we went out for ice cream. Nervous about the proposal I'd planned for the following day, I told Liz that I was feeling sick to my stomach.

She thought I had gas! Liz said, "You gotta put your butt up in the air—that releases the gas in your stomach."

"Uhhh..." I hedged. "Thanks. Maybe I'll try that later."

She clearly didn't know I was sick from *nerves* about proposing.

"It really works!" she promised.

The following day we drove to a quaint little town along Lake Michigan called South Haven and sat beside a thick red lighthouse at the end of a pier. I'd gathered photos from throughout our relationship, including one from our first date six months earlier, and I'd purchased a plaque we'd admired that read: "Love takes us to unexpected places but love brings us home." The gifts, the ring, and a note I'd written to Liz were tucked inside the blue velvet interior of my guitar case. I'd suggested to her that since we'd missed church that morning to drive to South Haven, we could sit near the water and sing some songs.

Sitting on the edge of the pier, feet dangling in the cold lake, I reached for my guitar case, opening it carefully so Liz wouldn't see the treasures inside. We sang a song called "Oceans," about having faith in and being led by God. A little crowd gathered around us as if we were performing just for them.

I told Liz I had a little gift for her, and offered the picture-story of our relationship, the plaque, and then the letter about what she meant to me. While she was reading it, I hopped up and dug the ring out of the pouch in my case meant to hold guitar picks.

When Liz looked up and saw me kneeling in front of her, she stopped kicking her bare feet in the water and emotion filled her face.

"Thank you," she said, gesturing toward the picture book. "This means so much."

With my heart racing, I looked in her eyes and asked, "Liz Wright, will you marry me?"

"Yes!" she said, rising to stand. "Yes, yes, YES!"

The last few "yeses" were so forceful that they hurt my ears.

When I'd dropped down on one knee, the same onlookers that had listened to us singing were once again alerted that something special was happening. When Liz jumped up and said yes, the crowd erupted in applause.

Four months later, on November 14, we were married at a local wedding barn in front of our family and friends. Many of them had prayed for me and supported my family after the accident. Liz and I had agreed that we wanted our first dance to be to Mark Cohn's "True Companion." What she didn't know was that about five seconds into the original track, the DJ was going to scratch it and begin playing the version of the song I'd recorded just for her.

Cuz, you know, that's how I roll.

Three months after our wedding, Liz and I were still feeling the big love. The honeymoon was *not* over. On Valentine's Day I took her to Mesh, a fancy restaurant in downtown Indianapolis. After being seated by the maître d' and browsing through the menu, I noticed a couple sipping wine across the way.

"Babe," I whispered, wide-eyed, "guess who's here?"

It was ridiculous to be whispering, because the couple I'd seen were seated across a loud, bustling restaurant.

Teasing me, Liz loud-whispered back, "I don't know! Who's here?"

"Shelly!" I said. "Remember I told you about Shelly, who I dated sophomore year? And all those things she said in the breakup letter?"

"Yeah," Liz said, "where is she?"

"Well," I said, cautiously, "don't be obvious, but if you turn around 180 degrees, it's the second booth from the door, and she's wearing a pink dress."

Slowly, ever so casually, Liz turned around to eyeball the one who got away. Glancing a few other places, like she was trying to spot someone else, she really nailed the nonchalant glance.

"She looks nice," Liz said. "You think that's her husband?"

"Yeah, I did hear that she got married."

"How you doin', babe?" Liz asked. "You okay?"

I paused to consider her question. As I paid attention to my body, I noticed that the heavy pain I'd carried years earlier from that breakup was completely gone.

With a smile I confirmed, "Yeah, I'm good. I'm *really* good."

As Liz and I returned to our menus, I had a strong sense that God was there at Mesh with me. And in my deep places I was reminded that He had always had a good plan for me, even in the moments when it hadn't felt that way.

CHAPTER 23

WHEN IT GETS REAL

I'd returned to Indiana hoping to see three areas of my life flourish: music, career, and dating that would lead to marriage. While God gave me more than I could ask or imagine in Liz, I was not flourishing in my career or music ministry.

When Liz and I married, I was working for Stanley Black & Decker as a channel marketing manager. But the marketing work was so similar to the Campbell's Soup Company position that it hadn't ever felt like the right fit, and the same thing happened—I was terminated. Somehow I was reliving the lesson I thought I'd learned when I transitioned from Campbell's to the Crocs store at the mall, shifting from marketing to sales. In fact, the boss who let me go confirmed, "You need to get a job in sales, because the reason you got this job is because you sold yourself." Her words stuck with me; I knew she was right. I was wired for sales, not marketing.

A couple weeks after I'd lost my job, Liz took a pregnancy test. Seeing just one pale line, she tossed the test stick onto the bathroom counter and told me it was negative. I was disappointed, but because I didn't have a job, I was also relieved.

When I went into the bathroom fifteen seconds later I glanced at the test, noticing a faint second line.

"I guess it's a dud," I called back to Liz. "There's like a super faint double line."

"What?!" she screamed.

When she explained that meant she was 100 percent pregnant, we both started jumping up and down with excitement. Liz wasn't scheduled to work that day and I was unemployed. Not quite sure what to do with ourselves, we went to the park to take a walk. It had been raining earlier in the day, but the sun was shining. We stopped by Target on the way home to buy a onesie to present to my mom to let her know she was going to be a grandma. In the parking lot, we were greeted by the sight of a bold rainbow stretching across the sky. I knew the literal "rainbow moment" was for us.

As excited as I was to welcome a child into our family, I was more than a little concerned about not being able to support us. Not only was my career in the proverbial toilet, but both my musical dreams of leading worship professionally and producing and selling the Kinney capo were stalled. During our walk that anxiety was simmering even as Liz and I celebrated and began to dream of the future we'd build as a family. But when I saw that rainbow, I was reminded once again of God's promise to Noah: "I have set my rainbow in the clouds, and it will be the sign of the covenant between me and the earth" (Genesis 9:13). God had preserved

Noah's family in the midst of a storm that flooded the earth, and God would provide for my family as well.

Because I'm human, there were of course moments when that peace escaped me. I was in the middle of mowing the lawn one evening at the house we were renting when panic gripped me. *How can I provide for Liz and our child? What will happen to us? Can we survive this?* While my anxious heart raced, I forced myself to put one foot in front of the other. Then I began to sing "It Is Well with My Soul." On repeat. *Acapella.* For an hour. I chose the truth of what I knew about God's faithful provision over the insistent pounding of the enemy's lie that He would not provide. Refusing to be bullied by my feelings, I declared my faith in the One I knew to be faithful and true.

CHOOSE TRUTH

When we face life's unexpected challenges—or when, as the song says, "sorrows like sea billows roll"—we can refuse to sink into the stormy seas of fear that threaten to overwhelm. In every moment we can choose what is most real. While it was true that I needed to pay the rent and put food on the table, what was most real was that the God who was a good Provider could and would meet our needs. While a terminal diagnosis is real, what is most real is that in life and in death our lives are in God's hands. Or while the agony of watching a loved one battle substance abuse is real, what is most real is that God loves him or her more than we can imagine and continually offers freedom.

> Whatever you are facing today, know that you have a
> choice. You can choose to let your mind focus on the fear.
> The grief. The anger. Or you can tip your eyes toward Heaven
> and lean into the truth: the reality that the gracious Lover of
> your soul is with you and for you when sea billows roll.

Pushing the mower back into the shed, I breathed a deep sigh of submission. I'd put my trust in God and believed that He would provide. As I stowed the mower, I noticed a cardboard box of childhood memorabilia that my mom had given me when Liz and I set up our first home. I'd been meaning to sort through it to decide what I wanted to keep, and without a day job, the moment was right.

On top was a picture of my soccer team from when I was nine. Then I found my second-grade school picture; my grin shows I'm grinning missing two front teeth. And there was a photo of me playing my parents' upright piano that had been salvaged from a church fire. While I had been the main piano player in our household, my mom often would play from an ancient brown hymnal when she was sad or stressed. After my accident I played a lot, which was therapeutic. And when the Sorums visited, even Pat played it as a stress reliever, like my mom and I did. That piano, which Liz and I have now, has been an important companion to all of us through our most difficult days.

Under the photographs was a certificate penned in calligraphy, mounted in a glass frame. Knowing there was a letter taped to the back of it, I fished it out of the box and sat down on a nearby patio chair to reread both. During the fall of my twelfth year, my dad and I participated in a weekend retreat for fathers and sons to mark the boy's transition into manhood. At twelve, I had taken that weekend together seriously. When I was given quiet time I wrestled with questions about who I was made to be: "What does it mean to be a man?" "What will my future purpose be?" "How will I help people?" "Will I be able to live up to being a man like my dad is?" Pretty big stuff for a twelve-year-old. I looked up to my dad in so many ways. He was a loving father and husband. He was a respected elder at our church. He ran a successful dental practice. I knew I wanted to be like him when I grew up.

When I was presented with the certificate at the end of the retreat, my dad shared a letter he'd written to me that I cherish to this day. It begins:

> *Every day you are closer to manhood and I am so proud of what I see happening in you.*

He named the qualities he saw developing in me: a heart for the Lord, confidence, personality, determination, work ethic, and the maturity of thinking before I speak. (Which likely signals that I needed to grow in that area!)

He continued:

> *Because I see these things in you and I see God's hand on your life and because I'm your father, I want to bless you and your future.*

He prayed that I would be wise in dating and marriage. That I'd be led by God's grace as I related to others. And he prayed that I would sense God's protection, direction, and delight in me.

Those words meant the world to me when I was twelve, having no idea what my future would hold. Upon this reading, though, I heard his heart for me, his prayers for me, through the lens of my accident and the family I was building with Liz. Words I'd skimmed past at twelve leapt off the page:

> *We are only beaten when we don't get up one more time.*
> *Life will bring many challenges. This attitude of deter-*
> *mination will be a great asset.*

My dad's words returned to me at the moment I needed them most. By then, I knew well what it was to get back up. I knew what it was to meet challenges with determination. And this moment was no different. I still didn't know how I would provide for my family, but as I looked at my situation through my dad's eyes, I knew God would continue to guide and provide.

I was still looking for work during Liz's second trimester. One evening when she clocked out for the day, I stopped by the salon to pick her up for a bargain date night at Chick-fil-A. We'd actually scheduled the pickup to coincide with her last appointment for the day—a patent attorney, Russ, whom we hoped could help me to advance my dream of sharing the Kinney Capo with the world.

We chatted a bit so Russ could learn more about my invention and get a sense of our budget. Since I was unemployed, that was close to nothing.

Russ generously offered, "I want you to research one hundred patents and learn how to write one for your capo. You take your best shot at writing it and I'll put the finishing touches on it for a minimal fee."

"Minimal," I learned, was a thousand dollars, which was well below what his services were worth. As the bells on the salon door jangled, signaling Russ's exit, I breathed a deep sigh of gratitude knowing I was one step closer to realizing the dream God had given me.

After that day I spent countless hours researching patents, then invested untold more hours into drafting one specifically by describing the ways that the Kinney Capo was unique from the others I'd studied. Russ also introduced me to someone who could produce a sketch of the capo for the patent. That drawing was spectacular. Then the artist introduced me to a talented robotics engineer who executed a computer-assisted drawing for the proto-type. But while the steps forward were exciting, our money was drying up quickly.

In that season I continued to nurture my dream of leading worship. During Liz's first trimester I'd auditioned for a job at one of Northview's satellite campuses. Three days later I heard from the director of music ministries that I wasn't the right stylistic fit for the position and that I needed more experience leading teams behind the scenes.

But there was one other exciting possibility bubbling: the opportunity to audition for a worship leader position at a vibrant church in Seattle. Ultimately, although the hiring team liked both me and my music, in the end I received a phone call letting me know I hadn't gotten the job. They said I didn't have enough experience.

Two doors had closed, forcibly, on the dream of leading others in worship. The timing was undeniably clear.

After the call with the church in Seattle, I shared the news with Liz and let her know I was going to go to Northview and spend a few hours in the chapel.

I parked my truck just a few spaces from where I'd usually parked in front of the Barn during high school, when peers and adults were certain I'd end up leading worship professionally. Knowing the church would be open for evening meetings, I walked in and headed toward the chapel. With its soaring ceilings, wood-paneled walls, and seating for two hundred, the chapel was taller than it was wide. I settled into the familiar space and let the tears flow.

Setting my guitar case on the red velvet cushion of the front-row pew, I pulled out my guitar and began to strum. Making music was often where I met God, and I longed to receive any kind of understanding about why my dreams weren't being realized.

I sang a few worship songs to get my heart right and then set down my guitar to speak to the Lord about releasing my dream of leading worship professionally. Closing my eyes, I spoke to Him in the quiet of my heart.

Is this what You want from me?

Do You want me to walk away from leading music?

Do You want me to step away even from volunteering as a leader?

I noticed a surprising sense of peace beginning to rest on me. When I opened my eyes I looked up to see a stained-glass window I'd looked at countless times during the decades I'd been at Northview, but had never really noticed until that moment. In response to the instruction to sacrifice Isaac, the son promised by God, Abraham is holding the dagger with which he is prepared to take the life of his child. Seeing Abraham's willingness to hold nothing back from the Lord, God stops him and provides a ram to sacrifice as a burnt offering instead of Isaac.

The scene is iconic, representing so many lesser moments in our lives when we long to be faithful to God and yet can't see how any good can come from our obedience. And yet I knew God was meeting me in that chapel and giving me peace about the disappointments I'd faced. I still believed my dream of leading worship professionally was from Him, so releasing it felt absolutely counterintuitive. And yet there was Abraham, whom God had called to be father of many nations. He trusted God so thoroughly that he was willing to let go of the son for whom he'd begged. If Abraham could let go, trusting God to provide what was needed, then so could I.

When I returned home that evening, Liz was surprised that the frustrated and disappointed guy who'd left earlier had been replaced by someone who'd encountered God's gracious presence.

As I continued to hunt for work, I'd been helping a friend's family get some leads for their real estate business. I didn't hate it, and wondered if that might be the right fit for me and my gifts. In fact, the family even helped pay my real estate licensing exam fees, which I failed the first time. And then a second time. And then a third.

While I was studying to take the test a fourth time, I received a call to interview with Fischer Homes, a new construction company in Indianapolis.

After my first interview with Fischer, I knew that both the company and its culture were a great fit—and my first weeks on the job confirmed it. I discovered I could really help people imagine the kind of home that would best meet their needs. The only downside of the position was that working weekends precluded continuing to serve as a volunteer worship leader at Northview. The peace God had given me in the chapel, however, continued to sustain me. I released the role with the confidence that a season had ended and a new one—in which I got to use the gifts God had given me to provide for my growing family—had begun.

Two months after I began working with Fischer Homes, Liz and I welcomed Jack Michael Kinney into our home and our hearts. Two years later we welcomed Henry Wayne Kinney. Both caused us to thank the Giver of all good gifts.

CHAPTER 24

CONTINUING TO LIVE
MY PURPOSE

At seventeen, two weeks after my car accident, I had been scheduled to attend a men's retreat where I was supposed to give a talk about being called to discipleship. My dad attended in my stead, speaking from my notes. Although I was disappointed to miss the retreat, that turned out to be a special ministry Dad and I shared. Afterward, he gave me the cross he was wearing around his neck when he delivered my words.

When Henry was an infant, I was invited to serve as an assistant director for the same men's retreat that had been so meaningful to me throughout my life. That year, it was scheduled for the first weekend of November, and the talk I was assigned to give was titled "Designed for God's Purpose." As so often happens when we share God's Word with others, the message that each man has been uniquely designed by God for a purpose only he can fulfill was exactly what God wanted to reveal to *my* heart in that moment.

Afterward, we entered a time of prayer and confession. As everyone prayed silently, God gave me a vision. Unlike the dream of the capo, in which He showed me something that did not yet exist, I was being shown a moment in time that shone beyond that one, seemingly into eternity.

I saw my friend Matt kneeing beside my unconscious body in the soybean field. His left hand was on my chest and his right hand was raised to the sky. It's important for me to say that even though this was the image on the "Used by God" rings that my dad had given to us, there was a way in which I had never really connected that message with my own sense of purpose. Matt? Yes, of course. But me? Somewhere inside, a part of me felt more like the object God used than a person with a purpose.

When Dad had first given me the ring it represented, to me, a moment in time when I rose from the ashes. So it had meant the world to me. But in the years that followed, I had doubts about how God could use me, given my brain injury and narcolepsy. I felt limited. I *was* limited. And that's why the capo gave me so much hope; it *removed* limitations.

In advance of that retreat, I'd been reading Rick Warren's book, *The Purpose Driven Life*. It had been released not long before my accident and although I'd seen it lying around my parents' home, I'd never read it. But as I dug into the book and ministered to the men on the retreat, something changed. The vision God gave me took me back to a spot in the soybean field where it had all started. In that moment in the chapel, the vision God gave me was no longer an image on a ring. Instead, I was kneeling right next to Matt and I heard God say, "This is why you are here, Mike."

The words God spoke to my heart both confirmed what He had done for me in that moment and fueled my mission in life.

This is why you are here, Mike. This is what I did for you by dying on the cross, and it's what I want you to do as My hands and feet. Trust God and pray for people who are lost and hurting and broken. Pray for those who feel all alone. Share the good news of My love and saving grace with them. That is why you are here, and My power lives in you. The same power that raised Me from the dead now lives in you. I am with you.

I.

Am.

With.

You.

Those four words resonated in my heart and came to rest, once again, in my deep places.

When I meet those who've suffered their own fiery ordeals, I am often invited to share the good news of God's love with them as well as the surety of His presence. But those who need to receive that true word aren't always gathered on a men's retreat. They may not be in an audience of worshipers. They're not necessarily marked in obvious ways as being "hurt" or "broken" or "alone." A few of the ones to whom I'm called live right under my own roof.

Each night at bedtime, Liz and I sing to Jack and Henry.

As we tuck Jack in, Liz sings "In My Life, Lord, Be Glorified." After saying a prayer for him I sing "Jesus Loves Me." Sometimes Jack joins us in song and other times he just lets the words wash over him as he wiggles or cuddles his raggedy stuffed bunny.

After Liz prays with Henry, I pray with him and sing "Twinkle, Twinkle, Little Star." Over his bed are the words from Joshua 1:9: "Be strong and courageous. Do not be afraid; do not be discouraged, for the LORD your God will be with you wherever you go." Since before he could speak, Henry would point to the words to ask me to read them for him. Though I'm keenly aware that he's usually eager to prolong the bedtime ritual, to postpone the inevitability of slumber, I gladly repeat them for him any evening he asks.

It's a Scripture I learned in Sunday School when I was not much older than my kids are now. Before any brain injury ever threatened my word recall, I was able to recite it for a chance at pulling a prize out of a grab bag. I usually focused on the "be strong and courageous" part, thinking about a fire fighter, a Marine, or Indianapolis Colts running back Marshall Faulk. And though I was able to parrot the part about God's omnipresence—"the Lord your God will be with you wherever you go"—I wouldn't linger there. Frankly, for a seven-year-old, that's a little boring.

But now, when I read those words for Henry as the sun sets outside his window, I know that my strength fails. My courage falters. There are absolutely moments when I'm afraid or discouraged. What does not fail—what cannot fail—is God's presence with me. God's presence with Henry. God's presence with Jack. Snuggled with a teddy bear under PAW Patrol sheets, at school, or in the fire. Today I know in my bones, due to circumstances I never would have chosen, that God is present in every moment of our lives.

Before we turn out the lights in our kids' rooms, Liz and I sing together the words God gave Moses to relay to Aaron and his sons to bless the Israelites: "May the Lord bless you, make His face shine upon you…" More than we want our sons to earn good grades, be popular, or succeed in their careers, we want them to know that God is with them. It is the song of our hearts for them because we believe it is the song of God's heart for us.

I have found such satisfaction in ministering to my boys through song. In some way it fulfills the dream God planted in my heart to lead others in worship that I never could have imagined. And while I'd released my dream of being employed as a worship leader before they were born, I had a niggling sense that God still wanted to use the dream He'd given me for the capo.

For eighteen months after I'd received that vision, I worked with my dad on a prototype. A business professor at Anderson saw its potential and asked what I'd do if he gave me $500,000. His encouragement inspired me, and for the years that followed I was never *not* ready to take the next step. My eyes and ears were open to see how God would provide.

When Liz introduced me to Russ, the attorney, I realized it was time for that next step: production. I was inspired, in part, by Pete Townshend's gift all those years earlier.

When I most needed hope, he had given me the Phoenix—a symbol of dying in the flames and being resurrected to new life. And I wasn't about to squander any part of my new life. In the season of recovery from my accident, I asked God to show me my purpose. So when I awoke in the wee hours following my nineteenth birthday with a vision that was not my own, I was given a very clear sense of meaning: I'd not been born anew from the ashes to live for myself, but to share my story, hope, and my gifts with others. And I had a very profound sense that one of the ways God was calling me to do that was to produce the capo.

DYING AND RISING WITH CHRIST

If the image of the Phoenix resonates in your heart in a primal way, it's because the "story" of dying and rising—and specifically a dying God—is recognizable across cultures and centuries. Twenty-four centuries before Christ, ancient Egyptian mythology refers to an ancient god named Osiris who was murdered. And twelfth-century Norse mythology tells how its chief god's son, Balder, dies as the result of an evil plot.

These are "types," but ultimately not stories that are *true*. In an essay called "Myth Became Fact," theologian and author C. S. Lewis acknowledges why these myths resonate as he points to the only one that became true:

"We pass from a Balder or an Osiris, dying nobody knows when or where, to a historical Person crucified (it is all in order) under Pontius Pilate. By becoming fact it does not cease to be myth: that is the miracle...God is more than a god, not less: Christ is more than Balder, not less."

Lewis encourages Christians not to be nervous about these cultural parallels, but to recognize them as pointing to something greater. In the 1993 film biopic *Shadowlands*, Lewis muses to his beloved wife, Joy, "What always stumped me was the sheer number of other dying-and-rising-god myths there were. I could never understand why our myth should happen to be the only one that was true." When Joy asks how he got unstumped, Lewis replies, "Well one day I thought, 'Maybe they're all true, all ways of telling the same story. What if there was just the one true myth that came to reality in Jesus Christ? All the other myths are merely echoes of it.'"

Pete Townshend's gift of the Phoenix echoes the story that is most true in human history, as does my own experience. Christ invites each of us to die with Him. And when we choose to join our lives to His, we are resurrected to a new kind of living—a life that really is life.

In early 2019, I arrived home from work to find a package waiting on the front porch. The return address declared it was from the United States Patent Office.

Catching my breath, I sat down on the stoop and opened the large manila envelope. The top page of the first stapled bunch of papers I pulled out was the cover page of the patent.

Tears instantly formed in my eyes. I was filled with a mix of excitement and relief. It was absolutely one of those "rainbow moments" that have confirmed for me the presence and goodness of God.

Though I was eager to share the patent with Liz and my boys, I knew there was something I had to do first. Dashing across the driveway to the garage, I pulled down dusty boxes from a shelf until I found a certain one. I set it on the ground and pulled open the four flaps that had been folded together. Digging through a stack of memorabilia from the season after my accident, I located the black picture frame that displayed the note Klancy had given me in high school.

More tears filled my eyes as I read the words that had been permanently etched on my heart: "Your story reminded me that God saved me for a reason...I thanked God for saving you and sending you to save me."

Klancy's note reminded me of the reason God had given me the dream of the capo in the first place. It certainly wasn't about me. It was, instead, an opportunity to reach others with the news of the One who died and rose.

Today I can see the many ways I get to live out God's purpose for my life. I am caring for Liz and our children. I am working in a job I love, helping people catch a vision for the home they want to build. I'm composing and performing the music God continues to plant in my heart. And I'm continuing to take steps to get the Kinney Capo into production.

But as passionate as I am about seeing this vision God has given me come to fruition, clamping a Kinney Capo to the neck of every guitar in the world won't be enough for me. I want people to know *why* it came to be. Yes, it gives beginning guitarists a way to perform one- and two-finger positions and experienced guitarists a way to experiment with new sounds. But what continues to drive me is so much bigger than that. For me, it's a symbol, like the phoenix. And my hope and prayer is that it inspires others to see Christ is present with them in the most difficult moments of their lives and to know that He's saving them for a purpose that is uniquely their own.

Maybe your purpose in this season is to care for an ailing family member. Maybe it is to launch a nonprofit. Or maybe your purpose in this season is to simply love your neighbors well. Whether you're right-brained or left-brained, an introvert or extrovert, a thinker or a doer, God has charged you with a unique purpose that only you can fulfill.

If you can see what that purpose is today, keep your eye on it. If it feels like more than you can manage, just take the next step to live it out. And if you can't yet envision it—if you squint your eyes but still can't quite see what God has for you to accomplish—pray and ask Him to show you. I assure you, it is a prayer that He *loves* to answer.

CHAPTER 25

UNWAVERING MELODY

The Sorum family visited us recently, and we all got to gather around my parents' kitchen table again just like we did when I was a kid. Except for the fact that we were eating hot, gooey pizza and my boys were running around like wild animals, it felt like one of the traditional Easter meals we used to share together.

Jamie was able to choke out a few words, but we needed Pat or Jim to translate the rough syllables. I fed Jamie, cutting the pizza into squares the way I did for Jack and Henry when they were still in high chairs. I kept a napkin in my left hand to wipe the saliva off her face after she struggled to chew each bite.

My boys were very interested in Jamie and her special chair with wheels. Because they're both concrete thinkers, with Jamie's permission and Pat's help I answered their queries about the chair, why her body shook, and why she needed help eating. When they get a bit older and their ability to think is more sophisticated, I look forward to telling them about my friend in the chair. I want them to know that the woman whose limbs were so shaky was still trusting God, even though she hadn't yet been rescued from her own burning truck.

Recently a film crew captured a slice of the Sorums' journey through Jamie's illness, her speech was slightly more intelligible than it is today—though Pat still needed to repeat her words to make sure they caught them. In that documentary, *Why She Smiles*, released in 2021, Jamie confirmed, "I'm fearless. I have no fear. I am going to die. I have found purpose because of my illness. There is a new peace. When my day comes, I'll be ready."

Her testimony brings me to tears. Jamie's trust in God's steadfast, loving presence with her doesn't depend on being rescued from the affliction to her earthly body the way I was. Daily she trusts in God's presence with her, even as her life is being robbed. She knows that He is near. She's received the promise He made to Joshua—the One He made good on in my life. And the promise on which Jamie has staked her life is the one God offers to you: "The LORD your God will be with you wherever you go" (Joshua 1:9). Yesterday, God was with you. Today, God is with you. Tomorrow, God will be with you.

Jamie's trust in God in the midst of smoke and flames is slightly different than mine. While some of us will be rescued from our burning trucks, others will experience redemption and healing when our bondage to these earthly bodies has ended. The reason Jamie has no fear of death is because she knows that Heaven awaits her. And when she imagines the new life she'll experience, where there are no more tears, no more shaking, no more suffering, she smiles.

As I wipe a dab of tomato sauce from her cheek, I breathe a silent prayer to God that my young boys will remember this woman who is fully confident, and fully alive, because she trusts in Him.

When we suffer, it's natural to look for meaning. The couple that battles infertility asks God, "Why?" The parents of a child diagnosed with leukemia beg, "Why?" The family of a man killed by a drunk driver ask, "Why?" The widow of a thirty-eight-year-old father of four asks, "Why?" Anytime we're living with circumstances we would not have chosen for ourselves, we wrestle to make sense of our experience.

And I believe that God wants us to ask those hard questions. He welcomes us to bring our confusion, sadness, anger, and fear to Him. And while we may not receive a satisfying answer about the "why," we can be confident that He never leaves or forsakes us in the fire.

This has become the song of my heart. Recently, God gave me and a friend words to the melody that's been pulsing inside me ever since my accident.

YOU ARE HERE

Here with one hand on my brother
And the other to the sky
I'm calling on the name of Jesus
To raise what's dying back to life
As I wait with expectation
My life surrendered to Your will
I believe Your ways are higher
You see beyond the pain I feel
In the fire I can see You

When my eyes can't see
Faith arise in me that You are here
You are here
Even in the flames I will praise Your name
You are here, You are here
You are with me in the battle
I'm surrounded by Your peace
Give me faith to move the mountains
Because Your power lives in me
When my eyes can't see
Faith arise in me that You are here
You are here
Even in the flames I will praise Your name
You are here, You are here
Even if it leaves me broken, I will follow where You lead
How I need You every moment
For You are strong when I am weak
God, I need You now
When my eyes can't see
Faith arise in me
That You are here
When my eyes can't see
Faith arise in me that You are here
You are here
Even in the flames I will praise Your name
You are here, You are here[1]

The circumstances you have endured in the past and the ones
you are facing today are unique. My prayer for you is that God will
shine light into any smoky, shadowy places in the story you've lived.

---

[1] Mike Kinney and Matt Siewert, "You Are Here," unreleased.

That He would strengthen your faith, and that you would encounter Christ in this moment and all others. Beloved, whether you find yourself caught in the fire today or whether you're living with burns and scars from the past, know that you are not alone. Jesus is lovingly, actively present with you in the flames and smoke.

He is with you.

Jamie's Homecoming

On January 17, 2022, Jesus picked Jamie up and carried her into Heaven. I imagine she is dancing now—dancing for joy and singing with her beautiful voice again, fully alive as she always was but without restraint. Jamie lived every day until the very end trusting that God is faithful. I will always remember Jamie's laugh and her smile. Her "against all odds" persistence to live her life to the full even as her earthly body and health deteriorated. Jamie went home before she could read *Out of the Fire* in its entirety, but her fingerprints are all over the book. She changed my life and my perspective in the years after the accident and helped me to see Jesus is always with us. We are never alone. Never forgotten. Never discarded. Never too broken to be used by God. We are His children, and He has a plan for each of us to accomplish His purposes until He calls us home.

I love you, Jamie. Thank you for showing me what it means to live through suffering. Thank you for showing me what it looks like to be strong and courageous even when we face life's greatest challenges. Your faith inspires me.

Acknowledgments

I am forever grateful to the many people who have helped me on this journey.

Jack, Henry, Merrill, Betsy, and Liz. John, Morgan, Rachel, Jim, Pat, Micah, Jacob, Lindsey, Margot, and Karla and Tim at Salem Publishing. Steve Arterburn and Steve Poe, Northview Church, and all those who have prayed for me.

Matt for being right there with me, and Jason for always answering my phone call. Mom and Dad for providing me a safe home as I grew up where I could learn and grow, make mistakes, and still know I am fully loved.

LET GOD SHOW YOU HIS PRESENCE IN THE FLAMES

Can you see God with you in your own fiery flames? When you close your eyes and return to the difficult moment or season in your own life, do you see the gracious face of Jesus? Can you hear His voice?

If the answer is yes, spend time with Him in that space. Go there in prayer and let Him minister to your heart. When old wounds flare up, return there and let Him care for you.

And if you haven't noticed Jesus with you in your pain, that's OK, too.

However, that doesn't mean He wasn't with you. It may simply mean that you've not paused to look and to listen.

For example, a friend of mine I'll call Sarah grew up in a household fraught with addiction and violence. As an adult, God was faithful to heal her heart by touching some of those early hurts.

When a friend invited Sarah to remember a moment of pain from her childhood, the one that popped into her mind was the night her parents announced they were getting divorced. She could see her family gathered in the dining room, and she saw her six-year-old self sitting in a straight-backed chair, hearing the news that her daddy was leaving their home.

And then Sarah's friend invited "adult Sarah" to prayerfully notice where Jesus was in the room. Eyes closed, searching for His presence, she noticed Jesus walking slowly around the family. He reached out to each person as He passed, offering comfort with His gentle touch. When He got to my Sarah, she saw Him lift her up and cradle her in his arms like an infant. As He held her, He allowed her to feel the sadness she'd been resisting, sharing it with her.

Jesus was present with Sarah by holding her in His loving arms. He was present with me by tending to my physical body. And He wants you to know, in your deep places, His presence with you in your most difficult moments.

Whatever concerns you carry, whatever challenges you face, whatever grief you bear, I encourage you to invite Christ to show you His nearness. Close your eyes and ask Him to show you where He was in your moment of need. Is He cradling you in His arms? Is He carrying a medical bag? Is He offering a listening ear? Is He offering you His hand?

Carve out time to be still with Jesus. Pray:

Father, thank You for the assurance that You never leave me or forsake me. Open the eyes of my heart to see Your face. Open the ears of my heart to hear Your voice. Come, Lord Jesus. Amen.